CONFIRMED
A Treasury of Faith & Prayer

*All documents are published
thanks to the generous support of the members
of the Catholic Truth Society*

CATHOLIC TRUTH SOCIETY
PUBLISHERS TO THE HOLY SEE

CONFIRMED
A Treasury of Faith & Prayer

Contents

6

The Effects of Confirmation
Unites us more firmly to Christ

Baptism is equivalent to birth; we are born of God, made sons and daughters of the Father in Christ Jesus. The complete renewal of our nature with the bestowal of the Spirit is given in baptism, in germ as it were. But the gift has to unfold and reveal all it contains gradually. The help of the Spirit is required here too, for growth in Christian life. Baptism gives us this treasure, confirmation, or rather the Holy Spirit, is the key that unlocks it. All is given in baptism; confirmation confirms, establishes, makes its deeper, firmer, extending it to the whole of our life. We live in time; God wills us to co-operate at each succeeding moment to bring about the full flowering of the initial gift.

By baptism we enter into God's family, we pass from death to life; we become living ones, alive in Christ; in confirmation we are life-giving. If baptism makes us sons and daughters of the Father in Christ Jesus, confirmation makes us witnesses and transmitters of this new life within us. By baptism we have put on Christ, been clothed with Christ that he may live in us; in confirmation we are made capable of spreading Christ.

By baptism we are called and justified, in order to be glorified (*Romans* 8:29). By confirmation we are sent to make disciples of all nations (*Matthew* 28:19); to this end we are clothed with power from on high (*Luke* 24:29).

By baptism we become disciples, among those who heard the word and put it into practice; in confirmation, we become prophets, possessing the power to witness to

Christ and bring truth to one's neighbour. Like baptism, confirmation confers a character; as an act of Christ and of his Church it cannot be repeated.

St Thomas Aquinas said that the character of baptism enabled the Christian to do whatever pertains to his own salvation. In the character of confirmation, Christians receive the power to attain spiritual perfection and fight temptation. "In this sacrament the Holy Spirit is given for strength; just as he was given to the Apostles on the day of Pentecost...the grace bestowed in this sacrament does not differ from that bestowed in baptism but increases what is already there."

"Go, therefore, make disciples of all the nations;
baptise them in the name of the Father and of the Son and of the Holy Spirit,"

(Matthew 28:19)

By the character, we are marked, as it were, by the ceremony and remain forever someone who has been confirmed. The character means we are marked, branded, we are possessed by God, or rather, disposed to being possessed. It is power, a talent for being a Christian that has to be developed. It is like the outline of a drawing, crying out to be coloured in. It brings with it a great capacity - for worship, prayer, the reception of the other sacraments. Or to use another analogy, it is like a muscle that wants to be used. In baptism and confirmation we have a muscle for living the Christian life. From this point of view there is no objection to giving the sacraments to infants and young children, for they will have within themselves the principle enabling them to act as witnesses of Christ when they develop.

This character is indelible; it cannot be effaced. That is why if someone is confirmed as a child or teenager, but later gives up his faith, he is still in potential a full member of the Church. He is like the prodigal son who left home without appreciating what a wonderful place it was to be. If later on he decides to return, the Church will welcome him back with the joy of the prodigal son's father: "Let us eat and make merry, for this my son was dead and is alive again" (*Luke* 15:23-24). The effects of the sacrament - boldness in confessing Christ, strength, responsibility for mission - may be blocked by our sin or unbelief, but given our collaboration, the character is a guarantee of that sacramental grace's abiding power.

Makes us "perfect" Christians
"After the font it remains for the perfecting to take place." *St Ambrose*

U puntil the ninth century the Rite of Confirmation was frequently called the rite of "perfection," completion or sealing. Confirmation has much the same meaning as when we refer to a business affair being signed and sealed: completed, finished, ratified. Confirmation is a perfecting or completing of the work begun in baptism. It confers grace beyond that already received and imparts a new sacramental character. But this completing or perfecting of baptism must be carefully understood. Baptism is complete and perfect in itself; nothing is lacking in it in terms of grace and salvation. The perfection of confirmation is a perfection of superabundance. Note how the *Catechism of the Catholic Church* uses comparatives when speaking of the grace of confirmation: "it roots us more deeply in the divine filiation…; it unites us more firmly to Christ; it increases the gifts of the Spirit in us; it renders our bond with the church more perfect" (*Catechism* 1303). Confirmation brings the superabundance of Pentecost.

It is a question of becoming more perfectly what we are already: children of God. The anointing at confirmation seals, makes safe, establishes the candidate in the Holy Spirit and, as the prayer for the Spirit over the candidates indicates, "completes" the process of initiation in which the Spirit has been active all along.

That's why it is said that confirmation makes us "perfect Christians"; it brings a "perfecting grace" that establishes a person fully in the Church, with all the responsibilities and privileges that entails. The word perfect can be misleading. In its primary sense it means completing, accomplishing, achieving something that has been begun. It is not primarily a perfecting of the candidate in the moral or psychological order, although, as in baptism and the Eucharist this is on the horizon.

The Eucharist perfects Confirmation

If confirmation perfects what has been bestowed in baptism, both baptism and confirmation are completed in the Eucharist. Confirmation's connection with the Eucharist is important. The Eucharist is the perfecting of both baptism and confirmation. These three sacraments form the Church's rite of initiation. As Aidan Kavanagh has remarked, "The most immediate vocation of the baptised and confirmed is to stand before God in worship at the Table."[1]

---

[1] *Confirmation: Origins and Reform* (New York: Pueblo, 1988), p. 87.

Baptism and confirmation prepare us for the Eucharist, and the Eucharist renews the grace of both. By celebrating the Eucharist we enter more fully into the mystery of Christ's death and Resurrection which we began to share at baptism; it also renews the anointing of confirmation, which is the personal Pentecost of each Christian. At each Mass we invoke the Holy Spirit, not only upon the gifts but also upon the people who receive them, renewing that full gift of the Spirit they received at confirmation. The dismissal at Mass is also an echo of our sending forth at confirmation to become messengers of Christ and heralds of the Gospel. Increasing the gifts of the Holy Spirit in us St Thomas Aquinas described confirmation as "the fullness of the Holy Spirit."[2] According to the *Catechism*, the main effect of the Sacrament of Confirmation is "the special outpouring of the Holy Spirit as once granted to the Apostles on the day of Pentecost." To be a complete Christian means the Holy Spirit guiding my life through his gifts. The Holy Spirit's personal name is Gift; he is the source of all gifts. "Come giver of gifts" we say in our Pentecost liturgy. The Spirit comes to give us gifts that have to be used.

When we think of the gift of the Spirit we might be tempted to think of gifts and graces that are unexpected, dramatic, spectacular - like the gift of tongues (where someone is given to speak about God in words he doesn't understand), or healing or miracle-working. St Paul does mention these. But he also speaks of the variety of functions in the Church as gifts: first apostles, second prophets, third teachers, helpers, administrators - all those things that build up the Church. As well as these institutional gifts there are the gifts of the Spirit:

---

[2] *Ibid.*, a.6.

the spirit of wisdom and understanding, the spirit of counsel and fortitude, the spirit of knowledge and piety, the spirit of the fear of the Lord. These gifts are already found in the prophet Isaiah (11:2).

The prayer before confirmation speaks of this sevenfold Gift with which the candidate will be endowed. The sevenfold gift also points to the way the Holy Spirit is ever ready to serve and help us. (That is why we speak of the Spirit as the "Paraclete," which is a Greek word for someone who comes to another's help, an advocate.) He helps us and serves us by giving us insight and understanding of the things of God, by giving us the strength for resolute and courageous witness, a strength that comes with abandoning ourselves to the strength of God; by filling us with a tender love and devotion for God. The seven gifts are really one: areas of activity in which the Spirit will make his presence felt.

As well as these seven gifts, St Paul speaks of the fruits of the Spirit: love, joy, peace, patience, kindness and goodness, faithfulness, gentleness, self-control. All this is what it is to live a life in the Spirit, to be a confirmed Christian. We will see the Spirit working in us when we see his fruits. To be a confirmed Christian is to use the gifts you are given for the good of all. Each believer has the right and duty to use these gifts in the Church and in the world. These gifts are to be sought and prayed for. Although we have become accustomed to speak of the seven gifts of the Spirit, the liturgy means the one gift, the gift of the Spirit himself. In confirmation we are given a particular grace to be open to the work of the Spirit, in the same way as Christ, Our Lady, and the Apostles opened themselves to the prompting of the Spirit and performed their work in the Spirit. The Sacrament of Confirmation is the sacrament of the mysterious influence of the Spirit upon the whole life of each Christian.

Perfects our bond with the Church

Through confirmation the baptised are "more perfectly bound to the Church".[3] The grace of confirmation should awaken "the sense of belonging to the Church."[4] Through baptism and confirmation we are enabled to make and become a self-gift to the Church for the good of the Church, and through her, for the whole world. The result is what tradition has called the *anima ecclesiastica*, the soul conformed to the Church, a soul which goes beyond its narrowness to embrace the dimensions of the mission of Christ and of the Church. The confirmed Christian grows in his consciousness of thinking with the Church and in the Church, of identifying himself or herself with the Church's intentions.

This ecclesial dimension of confirmation is important for any understanding of the sacrament. It is underscored by this sacrament's close association with the bishop, whether by allowing only the bishop to confirm, as has been the Roman practice, or by insisting that only chrism consecrated by the bishop could be used, as in the East.

Just as the Apostles after Pentecost imparted the Spirit by the laying on of hands, so the bishop does through confirmation. This practice "more clearly expresses the communion of the new Christian with the bishop as guarantor and servant of the unity, catholicity, and apostolicity of his Church, and hence the connection with the apostolic origins of Christ's Church" (*Catechism* 1292)

---

[3] The *Catechism of the Catholic Church* 1285; hereafter *Catechism*.
[4] *Catechism* 1309.

Confirmation thus strengthens one's bond with the bishop. The bishop is so closely involved because he is the successor of the Apostles who received the Spirit at Pentecost and the power to transmit the Spirit through the laying on of hands; and because he embodies in his own person the local church, and the wider Church. As far back as the second century, St Ignatius of Antioch expressed this conviction powerfully and succinctly: *"Wherever the bishop is, there let the people be, just as wherever Christ Jesus is, there is the Catholic Church."*

Although the bishop is the "original" and "normal" minister of confirmation, if the need arises, the bishop may grant the faculty of administering confirmation to a priest; priests may also confirm under extraordinary circumstances, as in missionary territories or in danger of death. Priests who baptise an adult or a child not baptised in infancy, or admit a baptised person into full communion with the church may also confirm, as these will receive baptism, confirmation and the Eucharist in one service.

Strength to be true witnesses of Christ

Baptism incorporates the individual into the Church which is the Body of Christ; confirmation brings with it a new factor, what the *Catechism* calls the "stricter obligation" of the confirmed "to spread the faith by word and by deed," to proclaim by a whole way of life the salvation won for the world by Jesus Christ. The Rite of Confirmation gives evidence of this in still another way. The laying on of hands found in the rite represents not only the outpouring of the Spirit; from the earliest days of the Church it has also been the sign of being established in ministry, of being sent on mission: "You will receive power from the Holy Spirit who will descend upon you. You will thus be my witnesses in Jerusalem, in all of Judea and Samaria, and unto the ends of the earth" (*Acts* 1:8). The same promise of Pentecost belongs as well to all those who are confirmed.

The work of the Spirit is to form us into another Christ who was sent out on mission from his Father. This does not mean all will be called to the missionary field; nor is it an invitation for all of us to change our jobs. To be an apostle, a witness, means to have a life, not a job. The first characteristic of apostolic life is sharing of the life of the Lord: Jesus summoned the Apostles "to be with him" and to be sent out to preach (*Mark* 3:14). Being with Jesus comes first and is the first mark of the apostle. They were called by him just to be with him; the fundamental law of any apostolate is union with Christ. Indeed, more than in external works, mission consists in making Christ present to the world through personal witness. This is the challenge, this is the primary task of the confirmed.

The more Christians allow themselves to be conformed to Christ, the more Christ is made present and active in the world for the salvation of all. Christians are "in mission" by virtue of their very consecration in baptism and confirmation; and they bear witness in accordance with their vocation in life. Like the Spirit himself, the confirmed Christian is at work everywhere, wherever he finds himself. St Paul himself was profoundly convinced of the fruitfulness not only of his work but also of his sufferings for the Church as a whole.

Indeed the most important acts exchanged in this communion are praying for others and suffering for others, since they are most closely linked to Christ's own being and acting for others. These things are at least as important as the external, visible mutual help and witness that is a matter of course for Christians.

> The real apostolate consists precisely in participation in the salvific work of Christ. Christ redeemed the world, a slave to sin, principally by prayer and the sacrifice of himself. In like manner, souls that strive to re-live this intimate aspect of the mission of Christ, even if they do not give themselves to any external activity, really contribute to the apostolate in an eminent manner (Pope John XXIII).[5]

Confirmation commits us to preaching, in one way or another, directly or indirectly, the mighty works of God.

If at confirmation we are given strength from on high to become witnesses of Christ, joy is one of the secrets of that strength. Those confirmed are anointed with the "oil of gladness". Pope John Paul II wrote an encyclical about evangelisation called *Redemptoris Missio*, and his final words in it point to the importance of joy in spreading the Gospel: "The characteristic of every

---

[5] *Allocution to Cistercian Abbots*, Rome, September 1962.

authentic missionary life is the inner joy that comes from faith. In a world tormented and oppressed by so many problems, a world tempted to pessimism, the one who proclaims the 'Good News' must be a person who has found true hope in Christ." Joy is given for witness.

Strength to defend the faith
"Reborn in baptism for life… confirmed after baptism for the strife"
(Faustus of Riez, 5th Century)

At his baptism, Our Lord was anointed by the Spirit for his work of proclaiming the good news. Immediately afterwards we find the Spirit leading him into the wilderness to do battle with the devil, whose work he was to destroy by miracles and healing, and ultimately by his death and Resurrection. At Pentecost itself there was such a strengthening; the first Christians became witnesses of Christ, spokesmen for his cause. Before Pentecost an Apostle could deny Christ; after it they were martyrs.

Martyr is the Greek word for witness. To bear witness to Christ is to encounter opposition, persecution, and often death. Included in the gift of Pentecost was the call to martyrdom. The light slap which used to be given on the cheek by the bishop after the anointing was a sign of the blows we must be prepared to endure for Christ. And the oil of the anointing recalls the anointing of athletes and wrestlers, with all its associated ideas of defence and strengthening. Confirmation shows martyrdom to be a universal vocation.

There is a constant tradition attributing to confirmation the grace of strength, especially for bearing witness even unto martyrdom, and for spiritual combat. In the fifth century St Cyril of Jerusalem exhorted his catechumens: "Just as Christ after his baptism and visitation by the Holy Spirit went out and successfully wrestled with the enemy, so you also, after your holy baptism and sacramental anointing, put on the armour of the Holy Spirit, confront the power of the enemy, and reduce it saying: 'I can do all things in Christ who strengthens me.'"

Confirmation makes us Christian soldiers. "This sacrament is given to man for strength in spiritual combat," noted St Thomas Aquinas. "Though he who is baptised is made a member of the Church, nevertheless he is not yet enrolled as a Christian soldier."[6] This is about something much more than the personal struggle of adolescents with which this sacrament is frequently associated; it concerns the ongoing struggle between the mystery of salvation and the mystery of iniquity (*2 Thessalonians* 2:7) which constitutes the secret history of the whole of humanity. Confirmation invites us to take seriously the realities of spiritual combat against the forces of evil in our time, against what St John Paul II called "the culture of death." It is a question of entering into the combat of Christ, with Christ. We have a powerful expression of the reality of spiritual combat in *The Lord of the Rings*, where it is seen that the one power before which evil is helpless is sacrifice, self-offering. Frodo, Gandalf and Aragorn are all in their different ways martyrs, Christ-figures who undergo different kinds of voluntary deaths and resurrections. In this kind of battle, strength is overcome by weakness,

---

[6] *Summa*, q.72, a. 9.

pride and power by humility, tyranny by martyrdom. In this world and the world of the Gospel, the self is only saved when it is lost, found only when given away in sacrifice. Sacrifice, humility, love, fidelity - these are shown to be the strongest, and most overlooked, weapons against evil.

We can recall too St Maximilian Kolbe voluntarily taking the place of another prisoner and going instead to die in his place. Christians today have particular reason to reflect on the centrality of martyrdom, for the century that has just come to a close has been pre-eminently an age of martyrs. In the twenty years between the two World Wars more Christians died for the faith than in the whole three hundred years after the crucifixion. Not all of us will be called to die outwardly for Christ in the gas chamber or prison camps; that depends on circumstances beyond our control. What we can do, however, is to be prepared to carry our cross inwardly. Clement of Alexandria affirmed that the true Christian will be a constant martyr: "He will be a martyr by night and a martyr by day, a martyr in his speech, his daily life, his character."[7] Confirmation is a call to life-long self-offering, not one of great self-sacrifices but a multitude of small ones: in the mutual love in marriage and family life, in acts of personal and community service, in loyalty to the teachings of the Church's magisterium and in defence of the faith.

What is essential in this is our fidelity to our Christian vocation. In both baptism, particularly in the rite of renouncing Satan, and in confirmation the Christian throws down a challenge to the forces of evil. This gives a meaning of love and redemption to the battles of everyday life.

[7] *Miscellanies* 2:20.

BASIC PRAYERS

Our Father

Our Father, who art in heaven,
hallowed be thy name.
Thy Kingdom come.
Thy will be done on earth as it is in heaven.
Give us this day our daily bread,
and forgive us our trespasses,
as we forgive those who trespass against us,
and lead us not into temptation,
but deliver us from evil.
Amen.

Hail Mary

Hail, Mary, full of grace, the Lord is with thee.
Blessed art thou among women,
and blessed is the fruit of thy womb, Jesus.
Holy Mary, Mother of God,
pray for us sinners,
now, and at the hour of our death.
Amen.

Glory be to the Father

Glory be to the Father,
and to the Son,
and to the Holy Spirit.
As it was in the beginning,
is now, and ever shall be,
world without end.
Amen.

I Believe (The Apostles' Creed)

I believe in God,
the Father almighty,
Creator of heaven and earth,
and in Jesus Christ, his only Son, our Lord,
who was conceived by the Holy Spirit,
born of the Virgin Mary,
suffered under Pontius Pilate,
was crucified, died and was buried;
he descended into hell;
on the third day he rose again from the dead;
he ascended into heaven,
and is seated at the right hand of God
the Father almighty;
from there he will come to judge the living
and the dead.
I believe in the Holy Spirit,
the holy Catholic Church,
the communion of saints,
the forgiveness of sins,
the resurrection of the body,
and life everlasting.
Amen.

Act of Faith

My God,
I believe in you and all that your Church teaches,
because you have said it,
and your word is true.

Act of Hope

My God,
I hope in you,
for grace and for glory,
because of your promises,
your mercy and your power.

Act of Charity

My God,
because you are so good,
I love you with all my heart,
and for your sake,
I love my neighbour as myself.

Commendation

Jesus, Mary and Joseph,
I give you my heart and my soul.

Jesus, Mary and Joseph,
assist me in my last agony.

Jesus, Mary and Joseph,
may I breathe forth my soul in peace with you.

Act of Resignation

O Lord, my God
whatever manner of death is pleasing to you,
with all its anguish, pains and sorrows,
I now accept from your hand with a resigned
  and willing spirit.

For the Faithful Departed

Out of the depths I cry to you, O Lord,
Lord hear my voice!
O let your ears be attentive
to the voice of my pleading.

If you, O Lord, should mark our guilt,
Lord, who would survive?
But with you is found forgiveness:
for this we revere you.

My soul is waiting for the Lord,
I count on his word.
My soul is longing for the Lord
more than watchmen for daybreak.
Let the watchman count on daybreak
and Israel on the Lord.

Because with the Lord there is mercy
and fullness of redemption;
Israel indeed he will redeem
from all its iniquity.

(Psalm 130)

V.   Eternal rest grant to them, O Lord.
R.   And let perpetual light shine upon them.
V.   May they rest in peace.
R.   Amen.

Let us pray:

O God, the Creator and Redeemer of all the faithful,
grant to the souls of your servants departed
the remission of all their sins,
that through our pious supplication
they may obtain that pardon which
    they have always desired;
who live and reign for ever and ever.
R. Amen.

For help

May the divine assistance remain always with us
✠ and may the souls of the faithful departed,
through the mercy of God, rest in peace.
Amen.

Prayer before a Crucifix

Behold, O kind and most sweet Jesus,
I cast myself on my knees in your sight,
and with the most fervent desire of my soul,
I pray and beseech you
that you would impress upon my heart
lively sentiments of faith, hope, and charity,
with a true repentance for my sins,
and a firm desire of amendment,
while with deep affection and grief of soul
I ponder within myself and mentally contemplate your
    five most precious wounds;
having before my eyes that which David spoke in
    prophecy of you,
O good Jesus: "They pierced my hands and my feet;
they have numbered all my bones".

MORNING &
EVENING PRAYER

Morning Prayer

V.   Lord, open our lips.
R.   And we shall praise your name.
Glory be to the Father... (Alleluia)

A hymn, suitable to the time of day or feast, may follow.

Psalm 99

(This or alternative psalms may be said)

Cry out with joy to the Lord, all the earth
Serve the Lord with gladness.
Come before him, singing for joy.

Know that he, the Lord, is God.
He made us, we belong to him,
We are the people, the sheep of his flock.

Go within his gates, giving thanks.
Enter his courts with songs of praise.
Give thanks to him and bless his name.

Indeed, how good is the Lord,
Eternal his merciful love.
He is faithful from age to age.
Glory be to the Father...

Scripture

(An alternative passage may be used)

You know what hour it is, how it is full time now for you to wake from sleep. The night is far gone, the day is at hand. Let us cast off the works of darkness and put on the armour of light; let us conduct ourselves becomingly as in the day. (*Romans* 13:11-13)

The Benedictus (Luke 1:68-79)

Blessed be the Lord, the God of Israel!
He has visited his people and redeemed them.
He has raised up for us a mighty saviour
in the house of David his servant,
as he promised by the lips of holy men,
those who were his prophets from of old.
A saviour who would free us from our foes,
from the hands of all who hate us.
So his love for our fathers is fulfilled
and his holy covenant remembered.
He swore to Abraham our father to grant us,
that free from fear, and saved from the hands
    of our foes,
we might serve him in holiness and justice
all the days of our life in his presence.
As for you, little child,
you shall be called a prophet of God, the Most High.
You shall go ahead of the Lord
to prepare a way for him,
To make known to his people their salvation
 through forgiveness of all their sins,
the loving kindness of the heart of our God
who visits us like the dawn from on high.
He will give light to those in darkness,
those who dwell in the shadow of death,
and guide us into the way of peace.
Glory be to the Father…

Intercessions

(These or other intercessions may be used)

Let us pray to Christ our Lord,
the sun who enlightens all people -

Lord our Saviour, give us life!
   (may be repeated after each line)

We thank you for the gift of this new day -

May your Holy Spirit guide us to do your will -

Help us to manifest your love to all those we meet -

Renew in us your gifts -

May we go forth in peace -

Our Father…

Concluding prayer

Almighty God, you have given us this day; strengthen
us with your power

and keep us from falling into sin,
so that whatever we say, or think, or do,
may be in your service and for the sake of the kingdom.
We ask this through Christ our Lord.
Amen.

✠ The Lord bless us, keep us from all evil and bring us to
everlasting life.
Amen.

Alternative personal prayers may include:

Our Father. Hail Mary. Glory be. I Believe.

Offering

O my God, I offer you all my thoughts,
words, actions, and sufferings;
and I beseech you to give me your grace
that I may not offend you this day,
but may faithfully serve you and do your holy will
    in all things.
I entrust myself completely to your boundless mercy
    today and always.

O Lord you have brought me to the beginning
of a new day.
Save me by your power so that I may not fall
    into any sin.
May everything I say, and all that I do,
be directed to the performance of your justice,
through Christ our Lord.

L ord, may everything I do begin with your
inspiration, continue with your help
and reach conclusion under your guidance.

Morning offering

O Jesus, through the most pure heart of Mary,
I offer you all my prayers, thoughts,
works and sufferings of this day
for all the intentions of your most Sacred Heart.

O most Sacred Heart of Jesus, I place all my trust in you.

O most Sacred Heart of Jesus, I place all my trust in you.

O most Sacred Heart of Jesus, I place all my trust in you.

During the Day

The Angelus

May be said morning, noon, and night, to put us in mind that God the Son became man for our salvation.

V. The Angel of the Lord declared to Mary:
R. And she conceived of the Holy Spirit.
   Hail Mary…

V. Behold the handmaid of the Lord:
R. Be it done to me according to your word.
   Hail Mary…

V. And the Word was made flesh:
R. And dwelt among us.
   Hail Mary…

V. Pray for us, O holy Mother of God.
R. That we may be made worthy of the promises of Christ.

Let us pray:

Pour forth, we beseech you, O Lord,
   your grace into our hearts,
that we, to whom the Incarnation of Christ,
   your Son,
was made known by the message of an Angel,
may by his Passion and Cross ✠
be brought to the glory of his Resurrection,
through the same Christ our Lord.
R. Amen.

(In Eastertime, the Angelus is replaced by the Regina Caeli)

Evening Prayer

V.   O God, come to our aid.
R.   O Lord, make haste to help us.
Glory be to the Father...

Hymn

A hymn, suitable to the time of day or feast, may follow, e.g.:

O Trinity of blessed light,
O Unity of princely might,
The fiery sun now goes his way;
Shed thou within our hearts thy ray.
To thee our morning song of praise,
To thee our evening prayer we raise;
Thy glory suppliant we adore
For ever and for evermore.
All laud to God the Father be;
All praise, eternal Son, to thee;
All glory, as is ever meet,
To God the holy Paraclete.
Amen.

Psalm 16
(An alternative psalm may be said)

Preserve me, God, I take refuge in you.
I say to the Lord: "You are my God.
My happiness lies in you alone".

He has put into my heart a marvellous love
for the faithful ones who dwell in his land.
Those who choose other gods increase their sorrows.
Never will I offer their offerings of blood.
Never will I take their name upon my lips.

O Lord, it is you who are my portion and cup;
it is you yourself who are my prize.
The lot marked out for me is my delight:
welcome indeed the heritage that falls to me!

I will bless the Lord who gives me counsel,
who even at night directs my heart.
I keep the Lord ever in my sight:
since he is at my right hand, I shall stand firm.

And so my heart rejoices, my soul is glad;
even my body shall rest in safety.
For you will not leave my soul among the dead,
nor let your beloved know decay.

You will show me the path of life,
the fullness of joy in your presence,
at your right hand happiness for ever.
Glory be to the Father...

Scripture

(An alternative passage may be used)

Let us give thanks to the God and Father of our Lord Jesus Christ, the merciful Father, the God from whom all help comes! He helps us in all our troubles, so that we are able to help those who have all kinds of troubles, using the same help that we ourselves have received from God. (*2 Corinthians* 1:3-4)

Magnificat (Luke 1:46-55)

My soul glorifies the Lord,
my spirit rejoices in God, my Saviour.
He looks on his servant in her lowliness; henceforth all ages will call me blessed.
The Almighty works marvels for me.
Holy his name!
His mercy is from age to age,
on those who fear him.
He puts forth his arm in strength
and scatters the proud-hearted.
He casts the mighty from their thrones
and raises the lowly.
He fills the starving with good things,
sends the rich away empty.
He protects Israel, his servant,
remembering his mercy,
the mercy promised to our fathers,
to Abraham and his sons for ever.
Glory be to the Father…

Intercessions

(These or other intercessions may be used)

May your kingdom of peace and justice
be realised on earth as in heaven -
Lord, hear our prayer.
> *(may be repeated after each line)*

Show yourself to all who seek you
in sincerity of heart -

Lord Jesus Christ,
light of all the nations,
shine upon those who walk in darkness
and in the shadow of death -

Be with all those who suffer in mind,
body or spirit -

Show mercy to the dead;
bring them to rejoice in the company
of the Blessed Virgin Mary
and all your saints -

Our Father...

Concluding prayer

Let our evening prayer rise before you
like incense, Lord, and may your blessing
shower down upon us: so that now and for ever your
grace may heal and save us.
We ask this through Christ Our Lord.
Amen.
✠ May the Lord bless us, keep us from all evil
and bring us to everlasting life.

Alternative personal prayers may include:
Our Father. Hail Mary. Glory be. I Believe.

O my God, I thank you for all the benefits
which I have ever received from you,
and especially this day.
Give me light to see what sins I have committed,
and grant me the grace to be truly sorry for them.
(A brief examination of conscience may follow)

O my God, because you are so good,
I am very sorry that I have sinned against you
and by the help of your grace I will not sin again.

On going to bed

Into your hands, O Lord, I commend my spirit:
Lord Jesus, receive my soul.
In the name of our Lord Jesus Christ crucified,
I lay me down to rest.
Bless me, O Lord, and defend me;
preserve me from a sudden and unprovided death
and from all dangers,
and bring me to life everlasting with you.

PRAYERS TO
THE HOLY SPIRIT

Veni Creator Spiritus

Come, Holy Spirit, Creator, come
from thy bright heavenly throne.
Come, take possession of our souls,
and make them all thine own.

Thou who art called the Paraclete,
best gift of God above,
the living spring, the living fire,
sweet unction and true love.

Thou who art sevenfold in thy grace,
finger of God's right hand;
his promise, teaching little ones
to speak and understand.

O guide our minds with thy blest light,
with love our hearts inflame;
and with thy strength which never decays,
confirm our mortal frame.

Far from us drive our deadly foe;
true peace unto us bring;
and through all perils lead us safe
beneath thy sacred wing.

Through thee may we the Father know,
through thee the eternal Son,
and thee, the Spirit of them both,
thrice-blessed Three in One.

All glory to the Father be,
with his co-equal Son;
the same to thee, great Paraclete,
while endless ages run.

Veni Sancte Spiritus

Come, Holy Spirit, come!
And from your celestial home
Shed a ray of light divine!

Come, Father of the poor!
Come, source of all our store!
Come, within our bosoms shine.

You, of comforters the best;
You, the soul's most welcome guest;
Sweet refreshment here below.

In our labour, rest most sweet;
Grateful coolness in the heat;
Solace in the midst of woe.

O most blessed Light divine,
Shine within these hearts of yours,
And our inmost being fill!

Where you are not, we have naught,
Nothing good in deed or thought,
Nothing free from taint of ill.

Heal our wounds, our strength renew;
On our dryness pour your dew;
Wash the stains of guilt away.

Bend the stubborn heart and will;
Melt the frozen, warm the chill;
Guide the steps that go astray.

On the faithful, who adore
And confess you, evermore
In your sevenfold gift descend.

Give them virtue's sure reward;
Give them your salvation, Lord;
Give them joys that never end.
Amen.

Prayer to the Holy Spirit

V.   Come, O Holy Spirit,
       fill the hearts of your faithful,

R.   and enkindle in them the fire of your love.

V.   Send forth your Spirit
       and they shall be created.

R.   And you shall renew the face of the earth.

Let us pray:

O God, who taught the hearts of the faithful
by the light of the Holy Spirit,
grant that by the gift of the same Spirit
we may be always truly wise and ever rejoice
   in his consolation.
Through Christ our Lord.
R. Amen.

PENITENTIAL
PRAYERS

Sacrament of Reconciliation

Remember that the sacrament is above all an act of God's love. It is a personal moment to be lived in a relationship of love with God. It is not routine, nor an ordeal to be gone through, but is very much part of the personal renewal which takes place in each person. You are invited, in the light of God's love, to recognise the sinfulness of your life, to have true sorrow for your sins, and a firm intention to avoid them in future.

Essential elements of a good confession

To make a good confession, we should:

1. Pray first, asking God to help us.

2. Make a sincere examination of conscience to see how we have sinned since our last confession.

3. Confess our sins simply, with humility and honesty.

4. Make our act of contrition with heartfelt sorrow and a "firm purpose of amendment", being determined that we will avoid the occasions of sin.

5. Devoutly carry out the penance prescribed and pray in thanksgiving for God's overflowing love and mercy.

Prayer before Confession

Almighty and merciful God,
you have brought me here in the name of your Son
to receive your mercy and grace
in my time of need.
Open my eyes to see the evil I have done.
Touch my heart and convert me to yourself.
Where sin has separated me from you,
may your love unite me to you again:
where sin has brought weakness,
may your power heal and strengthen;
where sin has brought death,
may your Spirit raise to new life.
Give me a new heart to love you,
so that my life may reflect the image of your Son.
May the world see the glory of Christ
    revealed in your Church,
and come to know that he is the one
    whom you have sent,
Jesus Christ, your Son, our Lord.
Amen.

The Confiteor

I confess to almighty God
and to you, my brothers and sisters,
that I have greatly sinned,
in my thoughts and in my words,
in what I have done and in what I have failed to do,
through my fault, through my fault,
through my most grievous fault;
therefore I ask blessed Mary ever-Virgin,
all the Angels and Saints,
and you, my brothers and sisters,
to pray for me to the Lord our God.

An Act of Contrition

O my God, I am sorry and beg pardon for all my sins,
and detest them above all things,
because they deserve your dreadful punishments,
because they have crucified
    my loving Saviour Jesus Christ,
and, most of all,
because they offend your infinite goodness;
and I firmly resolve, by the help of your grace,
never to offend you again,
and carefully to avoid the occasions of sin.

Examination of Conscience

Careful preparation is vital in order to make the most of this encounter with our loving heavenly Father. Find some time to be alone and quiet to reflect on your life, your relationship with God and others. An examination of conscience provides us with what we are going to say in the confessional. Without time given to such examination our confession is in danger of being incomplete. There are many ways: one is to use a Gospel passage, especially one of the many healing miracles or occasions of forgiveness (e.g. *Luke* 15:11-32; *John* 4:5-42; *Matthew* 18:21-35; *Luke* 18:9-14). Imagine you are the person being healed or forgiven by Jesus. Read the Scripture passage, imagine you are in the scene, and listen to the words of Jesus. He speaks to you! What do you say? Alternatively, Jesus summed up and extended the Ten Commandments by his two great commandments (*Mark* 12:28-42): love God and your neighbour.

Mortal sin is sin whose object is a grave matter and which is also committed with full knowledge and deliberate consent (*Catechism* 1857). We must confess all mortal sins. We are not obliged to confess all venial sins. We commit venial sin when, in a less serious matter, we do not observe the standard prescribed by the moral law, or when we disobey the moral law in a grave matter, but without full knowledge or without complete consent (*Catechism* 1862). Confession of venial sins is an act of devotion. We need not be unduly anxious to confess them all, but may rather choose to focus on areas of our life that are most in need of God's grace.

The following examination of conscience can help us to measure our lives by the objective standard of Christ's teaching. We may also consider more generally how we may have failed in our lives to live fully as Disciples of Christ.

Sins against God

- Have I rejected my faith, refused to find out more about it?

- Have I forgotten my daily prayers or said them badly?

- Have I experimented with the occult or put my trust in fortune tellers or horoscopes?

- Have I blasphemed against God or used bad language?

- Have I shown disrespect for holy things, places or people?

- Have I missed Mass on Sundays or Holydays through my own fault?

- Have I let myself be distracted at Mass or distracted others?

- Have I received Holy Communion in a state of mortal sin?

- Have I received Holy Communion without proper reverence, care or thanksgiving?

Sins against myself and others

- Have I been impatient, angry or jealous?

- Have I brooded over injuries or refused to forgive?

- Have I taken part in or encouraged abortion, the destruction of human embryos, euthanasia or any other means of taking human life?

- Have I been verbally or physically violent to others?

- Have I been racist in my thoughts, words or deeds?

- Have I hurt anyone by speaking badly about them?

- Have I betrayed confidences without good cause or revealed things simply to hurt others?

- Have I judged others rashly?

- Have I been drunk or used illegal drugs?

- Have I driven dangerously or inconsiderately?

- Have I spoken in an obscene way?

- Have I looked at obscene pictures, films or books?

- Have I been involved in any impure behaviour on my own or with someone else?

- Have I been vain, proud, selfish or self-seeking?

- Have I told lies to excuse myself, to hurt others or to make myself look more important?

- Have I stolen anything?
- Have I failed to contribute to the support of the Church in proportion to my means?
- Have I been disobedient, rude or insolent to those in authority over me?
- Have I been harsh, overbearing or sarcastic to those under my authority?
- Have I cheated my employers or employees?
- Have I misused or damaged the property of others?
- Have I set my heart greedily on possessing things?
- Have I given scandal or bad example?
- Have I been lazy at my work, study or domestic duties?
- Have I been jealous of others - of their looks, their popularity, their good work?
- Have I encouraged others to do wrong in any way?

For spouses

- Have I neglected to foster the warmth of my love and affection for my spouse?
- Have I prolonged disagreements through resentment or failing to apologise when I have been in the wrong?
- Have I mistreated my spouse verbally, emotionally or physically?
- Have I used artificial means of birth control?
- Have I been unfaithful to my spouse in any way?

For parents

- Have I neglected to teach my children to pray?

- Have I neglected the religious education of my children?

- Have I failed to bring my children to Sunday Mass?

- Have I argued with my spouse in front of my children?

- Have I failed to exercise vigilance over what my children read, see on television or on the internet?

- Have I been harsh or overbearing to my children?

- Have I neglected my children's welfare in any way?

For young people

- Have I been disobedient to my parents?

- Have I been unhelpful at home?

- Have I failed to try to understand my parents and talk with them?

- Have I upset the peace of my home for selfish reasons?

- Have I lost control when I have been angry?

- Have I sulked or been sarcastic instead of asking for help?

- Have I failed to work properly at school?

- Have I treated teachers or other adults with disrespect?

- Have I played unfairly at games or sports?

- Have I taken part in fights?

Going to Confession

(You may take this prayer book with you to Confession)

Reception

The priest welcomes the penitent warmly.
The penitent and priest begin by making the Sign of
the Cross, while saying:

✠ In the name of the Father,
and of the Son,
and of the Holy Spirit.
Amen.

The priest invites you to trust in God. You may indicate your
state of life, and anything else which may help the priest
as confessor.

The Word of God

The priest may invite you to reflect on a passage from Holy
Scripture, speaking of God's mercy and call to conversion.

Reconciliation

Then you can speak in your own words or you can say:

Bless me Father for I have sinned.
My last confession was … ago
(say roughly how long)
and these are my sins.

Now tell your sins simply in your own words.
When you have finished, let the priest know.
You can use these words if you wish:
I am sorry for all these sins and for any that I cannot
now remember.

*Listen carefully to the advice of the priest and ask the Holy
Spirit to help him to say what is best to help you to grow in
the Christian life. You can ask him questions if you want.
The priest may propose an Act of Penance, which should
serve not only to make up for the past but also to help begin
a new life and provide an antidote to weakness. It may take
the form of prayer, self-denial, and especially of service
to one's neighbour and works of mercy.*

Then the priest invites you to say a prayer of sorrow
(an *Act of Contrition*), such as:

O my God, because you are so good,
I am very sorry that I have sinned against you,
and by the help of your grace I will not sin again.

*Wait while the priest says the prayer of "Absolution"
(where Christ forgives you all your sins).*

Make the Sign of the Cross as the priest says:

I absolve you from your sins
in the name of the Father,
and of the Son, ✠ and of the Holy Spirit.
Amen.

*The priest may say a few final words of encouragement
to you as you leave.*

After Confession

*Take some time in the quiet of the Church to reflect on the
grace of the sacrament and to thank God for his mercy and
forgiveness. Here is a prayer of thanksgiving:*

Father, in your love you have brought me from
evil to good and from misery to happiness. Through
your blessings give me the courage
of perseverance. Amen.

The Way of the Cross

The Way of the Cross is a devotion to the Sacred Passion in which we accompany, in spirit, our Blessed Lord in his sorrowful journey from the house of Pilate to Calvary, and recall, with sorrow and love, all that took place from the time when he was condemned to death to his being laid in the tomb. We meditate devoutly on the Passion and Death of our Lord as we move around the stations in the Church.

Often, when made publicly, the following response is said at each station as we genuflect:

V.   We adore you, O Christ, and we praise you.

R.   Because by your Holy Cross you have redeemed the world.

The following act of contrition may be used at each station:

I love you, Jesus, my love above all things.
I repent with my whole heart of having offended you.
Never permit me to separate myself from you again.
Grant that I may love you always
and then do with me what you will.

Our Father; Hail Mary; Glory be.

I. Jesus is condemned to death

Consider how Jesus, after having been scourged and crowned with thorns, was unjustly condemned by Pilate to die on the Cross.

II. Jesus receives the Cross

Consider how Jesus, in making this journey with the Cross on his shoulders, thought of us, and offered for us to his Father the death he was about to undergo.

III. Jesus falls the first time

Consider the first fall of Jesus under his Cross. His flesh was torn by the scourges, his head was crowned with thorns; he had lost a great quantity of blood. So weakened he could scarcely walk, he yet had to carry this great load upon his shoulders. The soldiers struck him rudely, and he fell several times.

IV. Jesus is met by his Blessed Mother

Consider this meeting of the Son and the Mother, which took place on this journey. Their looks became like so many arrows to wound those hearts which loved each other so tenderly.

V. The Cross is laid upon Simon of Cyrene

Consider how his cruel tormentors, seeing that Jesus was on the point of expiring, and fearing he would die on the way, whereas they wished him to die the shameful death of the Cross, constrained Simon of Cyrene to carry the Cross behind our Lord.

VI. Veronica wipes the face of Jesus

Consider how the holy woman named Veronica, seeing Jesus so ill-used, and bathed in sweat and blood, wiped his face with a towel, on which was left the impression of his holy countenance.

VII. Jesus falls the second time

Consider the second fall of Jesus under the Cross; a fall which renews the pain of all the wounds in his head and members.

VIII. The women of Jerusalem mourn for our Lord

Consider how these women wept with compassion at seeing Jesus in such a pitiable state, streaming with blood, as he walked along. "Daughters of Jerusalem", said he, "weep not for me, but for yourselves and for your children".

IX. Jesus falls the third time

Consider the third fall of Jesus Christ. His weakness was extreme, and the cruelty of his executioners excessive, who tried to hasten his steps when he could scarcely move.

X. Jesus is stripped of his garments

Consider the violence with which Jesus was stripped by the executioners. His inner garments adhered to his torn flesh, and they dragged them off so roughly that the skin came with them. Take pity on your Saviour thus cruelly treated.

XI. Jesus is nailed to the Cross

Consider how Jesus, having been placed upon the Cross, extended his hands, and offered to his Eternal Father the sacrifice of his life for our salvation. Those barbarians fastened him with nails, and then, securing the Cross, allowed him to die with anguish on this infamous gibbet.

XII. Jesus dies on the Cross

Consider how Jesus, being consumed with anguish after three hours' agony on the Cross, abandoned himself to the weight of his body, bowed his head and died.

XIII. Jesus is taken down from the Cross

Consider how, after our Lord had expired, two of his disciples, Joseph and Nicodemus, took him down from the Cross and placed him in the arms of his afflicted Mother, who received him with unutterable tenderness, and pressed him to her bosom.

XIV. Jesus is placed in the sepulchre

Consider how the disciples, accompanied by his holy Mother, carried the body of Jesus to bury it. They closed the tomb, and all came sorrowfully away.

DEVOTIONAL
PRAYERS OF
THE CHURCH

The Divine Mercy

The devotion consists in the adoration of Mercy, the heart of which is trust, meaning to assume an attitude conforming to Jesus's will. Trustful believers are assured many graces in this world and eternal happiness in the next. The Novena of the Divine Mercy (which includes the Chaplet, and other prayers) begins on Good Friday and ends on Divine Mercy Sunday.

The Chaplet

Prayed on ordinary rosary beads, in the following order:

The Our Father, Hail Mary, Apostles' Creed.

On the large bead before each decade:

Eternal Father,
I offer you the Body and Blood,
Soul and Divinity of Your dearly beloved Son,
Our Lord Jesus Christ,
in atonement for our sins and those of the world.

Once on each of the ten small beads:

For the sake of his sorrowful Passion,
have mercy on us and on the whole world.

Concluding doxology

After five decades repeat three times:

Holy God, Holy Mighty One, Holy Immortal One, have mercy on us and the whole world.

O Blood and Water

O Blood and Water, which gushed forth from the heart of Jesus as a Fount of Mercy for us, I trust in you.

The Litany of the Divine Mercy

Divine Mercy,
gushing forth from the bosom of the Father,
I trust in you. (Repeat this after each line)

Divine Mercy, greatest attribute of God,

Divine Mercy, incomprehensible mystery,

Divine Mercy, fountain gushing forth from the mystery
of the Most Blessed Trinity,

Divine Mercy, unfathomed by any intellect,
human or angelic,

Divine Mercy, from which wells forth all life
and happiness,

Divine Mercy, better than the heavens,

Divine Mercy, source of miracles and wonders,

Divine Mercy, encompassing the whole universe,

Divine Mercy, descending to earth in the Person
of the Incarnate Word,

Divine Mercy, which flowed out from the open wound
of the Heart of Jesus,

Divine Mercy, enclosed in the Heart of Jesus for us,
and especially for sinners,

Divine Mercy, unfathomed in the institution of
the Sacred Heart,

Divine Mercy, in the founding of Holy Church,

Divine Mercy, in the Sacrament of Holy Baptism,

Divine Mercy, in our justification through Jesus Christ,

Divine Mercy, accompanying us through our whole life,

Divine Mercy, embracing us
    especially at the hour of death,

Divine Mercy, endowing us with immortal life,

Divine Mercy, accompanying us
    every moment of our life,

Divine Mercy, shielding us from the fire of hell,

Divine Mercy, in the conversion of hardened sinners,

Divine Mercy, astonishment for Angels,
    incomprehensible to Saints,

Divine Mercy, unfathomed in all the mysteries of God,

Divine Mercy, lifting us out of every misery,

Divine Mercy, source of our happiness and joy,

Divine Mercy, in calling us forth from nothingness
    to existence,

Divine Mercy, embracing all the works of his hands,

Divine Mercy, crown of all of God's handiwork,

Divine Mercy, in which we are all immersed,

Divine Mercy, sweet relief for anguished hearts,

Divine Mercy, only hope of despairing souls,

Divine Mercy, repose of hearts, peace amidst fear,

Divine Mercy, delight and ecstasy of holy souls,

Divine Mercy, inspiring hope against all hope.

Let us pray:

Eternal God, in whom mercy is endless and the treasury of compassion inexhaustible, look kindly upon us and increase your mercy in us, that in difficult moments we might not despair nor become despondent, but with great confidence submit ourselves to your holy will, which is Love and Mercy itself. Amen.

PRAYERS TO OUR LADY

The Holy Rosary

The Holy Rosary is composed of twenty "decades", each comprising the Our Father, ten Hail Marys, and the Glory be, recited in honour of some mystery in the life of Our Lord or his Blessed Mother. We pray to practise the virtue specially taught by that mystery.

I. The Five Joyful Mysteries
(Mondays, Saturdays)

1. The Annunciation. (*Luke* 1:26-38)

2. The Visitation. (*Luke* 1:39-45)

3. The Nativity. (*Luke* 2:1-7)

4. The Presentation in the Temple. (*Luke* 2:22-35)

5. The Finding of the Child Jesus in the Temple. (*Luke* 2:41-52)

II. The Five Mysteries of Light
(Thursdays)

1. The Baptism of the Lord. (*Matthew* 3:13-17)

2. The Marriage at Cana. (*John* 2:1-12)

3. The Proclamation of the Kingdom and call to conversion. (*Mark* 1:14-15; 2:3-12)

4. The Transfiguration. (*Luke* 9:28-36)

5. The Institution of the Eucharist. (*Matthew* 26:26-29)

III. The Five Sorrowful Mysteries
(Tuesdays, Fridays)

1. The Prayer and Agony in the Garden.
    (*Mark* 14:32-42)

2. The Scourging at the Pillar. (*Matthew* 27:15-26)

3. The Crowning with Thorns. (*Matthew* 27:27-31)

4. The Carrying of the Cross.
    (*John* 19:15-17; *Luke* 23:27-32)

5. The Crucifixion and Death. (*Luke* 23:33-38, 44-46)

IV. The Five Glorious Mysteries
(Wednesdays, Sundays)

1. The Resurrection. (*Matthew* 28:1-8)

2. The Ascension of Christ into Heaven. (*Acts* 1:6-11)

3. The Descent of the Holy Spirit. (*Acts* 2:1-12)

4. The Assumption. (*1 Thessalonians* 4:13-18)

5. The Coronation of the Blessed Virgin Mary.
    (*Revelation* 12:1; 14:1-5: *Isaiah* 6:1-3)

The Hail Holy Queen

Hail, holy Queen, mother of mercy;
hail, our life, our sweetness, and our hope!
To you do we cry, poor banished children of Eve; to you
do we send up our sighs,
mourning and weeping in this vale of tears.
Turn then, most gracious advocate,
your eyes of mercy towards us;
and after this our exile,
show unto us the blessed fruit of your womb, Jesus.
O clement, O loving, O sweet Virgin Mary.

> *V.*   Pray for us, O holy Mother of God.

> *R.*   That we may be made worthy of the promises
> of Christ.

Let us pray:

O God, whose only-begotten Son, by his life,
death and Resurrection,
has purchased for us the rewards of eternal life;
grant, we beseech you,
that meditating on these Mysteries of the most holy
Rosary of the Blessed Virgin Mary,
we may both imitate what they contain,
and obtain what they promise,
through the same Christ our Lord.
R. Amen.

Litany of the Blessed Virgin Mary

Lord have mercy.
Lord have mercy.
Christ have mercy.
Christ have mercy.
Lord have mercy.
Lord have mercy.
Christ hear us.
Christ graciously hear us.

God the Father of heaven, *have mercy on us. (repeat)*
God the Son, Redeemer of the world,
God the Holy Spirit,
Holy Trinity, one God,

Holy Mary, *pray for us. (repeat)*
Holy Mother of God,
Holy Virgin of virgins,
Mother of Christ,
Mother of the Church,
Mother of divine grace,
Mother most pure,
Mother most chaste,
Mother inviolate,
Mother undefiled,
Mother most lovable,
Mother most admirable,
Mother of good counsel,
Mother of our Creator,
Mother of our Saviour,
Virgin most prudent,
Virgin most venerable,
Virgin most renowned,
Virgin most powerful,

Virgin most merciful, *pray for us. (repeat)*
Virgin most faithful,
Mirror of justice,
Seat of wisdom,
Cause of our joy,
Spiritual vessel,
Vessel of honour,
Singular vessel of devotion,
Mystical rose,
Tower of David,
Tower of ivory,
House of gold,
Ark of the Covenant,
Gate of heaven,
Morning Star,
Health of the sick,
Refuge of sinners,
Comfort of the afflicted,
Help of Christians,
Queen of Angels,
Queen of Patriarchs,
Queen of Prophets,
Queen of Apostles
Queen of Martyrs,
Queen of Confessors,
Queen of Virgins,
Queen of all Saints,
Queen conceived without original sin,
Queen assumed into heaven,
Queen of the most holy Rosary,
Queen of the Family,
Queen of Peace.

Lamb of God, you take away the sins of the world,
spare us, O Lord.

Lamb of God, you take away the sins of the world,
graciously hear us, O Lord.

Lamb of God, you take away the sins of the world,
have mercy on us.

The Memorare

Remember, O most loving Virgin Mary,
that it is a thing unheard of,
that anyone ever had recourse to your protection,
implored your help,
or sought your intercession,
and was left forsaken.
Filled therefore with confidence in your goodness
   I fly to you,
O Mother, Virgin of virgins.
To you I come, before you I stand, a sorrowful sinner.
Despise not my poor words,
O Mother of the Word of God,
but graciously hear and grant my prayer.
Amen.

The Regina Caeli

V.   O Queen of heaven, rejoice! Alleluia.
R.   For he whom you did merit to bear, Alleluia,

V.   Has risen as he said, Alleluia.
R.   Pray for us to God, Alleluia.

V.   Rejoice and be glad, O Virgin Mary, Alleluia,
R.   For the Lord has risen indeed, Alleluia.

Let us pray:

God our Father, you give joy to the world
by the Resurrection of your Son,
our Lord Jesus Christ.
Through the prayers of his Mother, the Virgin Mary,
bring us to the happiness of eternal life.
We ask this through our Lord Jesus Christ, your Son,
who lives and reigns with you and the Holy Spirit,
one God, for ever and ever.
R. Amen.

PRAYERS FOR
VARIOUS NEEDS
AND OCCASIONS

Prayer of St Ignatius

Teach us, good Lord, to serve you as you deserve;
to give and not to count the cost;
to fight and not to heed the wounds;
to toil and not to seek for rest;
to labour and not to ask for any reward
save that of knowing that we do your will.
Amen.

Prayer of St Richard of Chichester

Thanks be to you, my Lord, Jesus Christ,
for all the benefits which you have given me,
for all the pains and insults
    which you have borne for me.
O most merciful Redeemer,
friend and brother, may I know you more clearly,
love you more dearly,
and follow you more nearly, day by day.
Amen.

Prayer to my guardian angel

O angel of God, my guardian dear
to whom God's love commits me here.
Ever this day/night be at my
side to light, to guard, to rule and guide.
Amen.

Prayer to St Michael

St Michael, the Archangel,
defend us in the day of battle;
be our safeguard against the wickedness
and snares of the devil.
May God rebuke him, we humbly pray and do you,
O Prince of the heavenly host, by the power of God,
cast into hell Satan and all the other evil spirits
who prowl through the world seeking the ruin of souls.
Amen.

Prayer for Life

O Mary, bright dawn of the new world,
Mother of the living
to you do we entrust the cause of life.
Look down, O Mother,
on the vast numbers of babies not allowed to be born,
of the poor whose lives are made difficult,
of men and women who are victims of brutal violence,
of the elderly and the sick killed by indifference or out
of misguided mercy.
Grant that all who believe in your Son may proclaim
the Gospel of life with honesty
and love to the people of our time.
Obtain for them the grace to accept that Gospel
as a gift ever new, the joy of celebrating it with
gratitude throughout their lives and the courage to
bear witness to it resolutely, in order to build, together
with all people of good will, the civilisation of truth
and love, to the praise and glory of God, the Creator
and lover of life.

(Pope St John Paul II)

In Temptation

Lord, save me, or I perish.
Keep me close to you by your grace,
or I shall sin and fall away from you.
Jesus, help me;
Mary, help me;
my holy Angel, watch over me.

In Trouble

In all things may the most holy, the most just,
and the most lovable will of God be done,
praised, and exalted above all for ever.
Your will be done, O Lord, your will be done.
The Lord has given, the Lord has taken away;
blessed be the name of the Lord.

In Sickness and Pain

Lord, your will be done;
I take this for my sins.
I offer up to you my sufferings,
together with all that my Saviour has suffered for me;
and I beg you, through his sufferings,
to have mercy on me.
Free me from this illness and pain if you will,
and if it be for my good.
You love me too much to let me suffer
    unless it be for my good.
Therefore, O Lord, I trust myself to you;
do with me as you please.
In sickness and in health,
I wish to love you always.

Prayer for Chastity

O my God, teach me to love others with
the purity of your holy Mother.
Give me the grace to resist firmly every
temptation to impure thoughts,
words or actions. Teach me always to love with
generosity and goodness, to respect myself and others
in the way I act and to reverence the way that you have
given us for the creation of new life.

In Thanksgiving

My God, from my heart I thank you for the many
blessings you have given to me.
I thank you for having created and baptised me, and for
having placed me in your holy Catholic Church; and for
having given me so many graces and mercies through
the merits of Jesus Christ.
And I thank you, dear Jesus,
for having become a little child for my sake,
to teach me to be holy and humble like you;
and for having died upon the Cross that I might have
pardon for my sins and get to heaven.
Also I thank you for all your other mercies,
most of all for those you have given me today.

Prayer for the Pope

O almighty and eternal God,
have mercy on your servant our Holy Father,
the Pope,
and direct him according to your clemency
   into the way of everlasting salvation;
that he may desire by your grace those things
   that are agreeable to you,
and perform them with all his strength.
Through Christ our Lord.
Amen.

Prayer for Priests

Father, you have appointed your Son
Jesus Christ eternal High Priest.
Guide those he has chosen to be ministers
of word and sacrament and help them to be faithful
in fulfilling the ministry they have received.
Grant this through our Lord Jesus Christ, your Son,
who lives and reigns with you and the Holy Spirit,
one God, for ever and ever.
Amen.

Prayer for Vocations

Lord Jesus Christ, Shepherd of souls,
who called the Apostles to be fishers of men,
raise up new apostles in your holy Church.
Teach them that to serve you is to reign:
to possess you is to possess all things.
Kindle in the young hearts of our sons and daughters
    the fire of zeal for souls.
Make them eager to spread your kingdom on earth.
Grant them courage to follow you,
who are the Way, the Truth and the Life;
who live and reign for ever and ever.
Amen.

Mary, Queen of the Clergy, pray for us.
Help our students who are preparing for the priesthood.

Prayer for Others

O Jesus, have mercy on your holy Church;
take care of her.
O Jesus, have pity on poor sinners,
and save them from hell.
O Jesus, bless my father, my mother,
my brothers and sisters,
and all I ought to pray for,
as your Heart knows how to bless them.
O Jesus, have pity on the poor souls in purgatory
    and give them eternal rest.

Prayer for Christian Unity

Look mercifully, Lord, on your people,
and pour out on us the gifts of your Holy Spirit.
Grant that we may constantly grow
    in love of the truth,
and seek the perfect unity of Christians
    in our prayers and our deeds.
Through Christ our Lord.
Amen.

Prayer for Peace

O God, from whom are holy desires,
right counsels and just deeds,
give to your servants that peace
    which the world cannot give;
that we may serve you with our whole hearts,
and live quiet lives under your protection,
free from the fear of our enemies.
Through Christ our Lord.
Amen.

THE ORDER
OF MASS

Introductory Rites

The faithful dispose themselves properly to celebrate the Eucharist.

Before Mass begins, the people gather in a spirit of recollection, preparing for their participation in the Mass.

All stand during the entrance procession.

Sign of the Cross

After the Entrance Chant, the Priest and the faithful sign themselves with the Sign of the Cross:

Priest:	In the name of the Father, and of the Son, and of the Holy Spirit.
Response:	**Amen.**

Greeting

The Priest greets the people, with one of the following:

1. Pr. The grace of our Lord Jesus Christ,
and the love of God,
and the communion of the Holy Spirit
be with you all.

2. Pr. Grace to you and peace from God
our Father and the Lord Jesus Christ.

3. Pr. The Lord be with you.

The people reply:

R.   **And with your spirit.**

The Priest, or a Deacon, or another minister, may very briefly introduce the faithful to the Mass of the day.

Penitential Act

There are three forms of the Penitential Act which may be chosen from as appropriate.

Pr. Brethren (brothers and sisters),
let us acknowledge our sins,
and so prepare ourselves to celebrate
the sacred mysteries.

A brief pause for silence follows.

Then one of the following forms is used:

1. **I confess to almighty God
and to you, my brothers and sisters,
that I have greatly sinned,
in my thoughts and in my words,
in what I have done and in what
I have failed to do,**
(*and, striking their breast, they say:*)
**through my fault, through my fault,
through my most grievous fault;
therefore I ask blessed Mary ever-Virgin,
all the Angels and Saints,
and you, my brothers and sisters,
to pray for me to the Lord our God.**

2. **Pr.** Have mercy on us, O Lord.
R. **For we have sinned against you.**

Pr. Show us, O Lord, your mercy.
R. **And grant us your salvation.**

Invocations naming the gracious works of the Lord may be made, as in the example below:

3. Pr. You were sent to heal the contrite of heart:
Lord, have mercy.   *Or:* Kyrie, eleison.
R. **Lord, have mercy.**   *Or:* **Kyrie, eleison.**

Pr. You came to call sinners:
Christ, have mercy.   *Or:* Christe, eleison.
R. **Christ, have mercy.**   *Or:* **Christe, eleison.**

Pr. You are seated at the right hand of the Father
to intercede for us:
Lord, have mercy.   *Or:* Kyrie, eleison.
R. **Lord, have mercy.**   *Or:* **Kyrie, eleison.**

The absolution by the Priest follows:

Pr. May almighty God have mercy on us,
forgive us our sins,
and bring us to everlasting life.
R. **Amen.**

*The Kyrie, eleison (Lord, have mercy) invocations follow,
unless they have just occurred.*

Pr. Lord, have mercy.   **R. Lord, have mercy.**
Pr. Christ, have mercy.   **R. Christ, have mercy.**
Pr. Lord, have mercy.   **R. Lord, have mercy.**

Or:

Pr. Kyrie, eleison.   **R. Kyrie, eleison.**
Pr. Christe, eleison.   **R. Christe, eleison.**
Pr. Kyrie, eleison.   **R. Kyrie, eleison.**

The Gloria

On Sundays (outside of Advent and Lent), Solemnities and Feast Days, this hymn is either sung or said:

Glory to God in the highest,
and on earth peace to people of good will.
We praise you,
we bless you,
we adore you,
we glorify you,
we give you thanks for your great glory,
Lord God, heavenly King,
O God, almighty Father.

Lord Jesus Christ, Only Begotten Son,
Lord God, Lamb of God, Son of the Father,
you take away the sins of the world, have mercy on
us; you take away the sins of the world,
    receive our prayer;
you are seated at the right hand of the Father,
have mercy on us.

For you alone are the Holy One,
you alone are the Lord,
you alone are the Most High,
Jesus Christ,
with the Holy Spirit,
in the glory of God the Father.
Amen.

Glória in excélsis Deo
et in terra pax homínibus bonæ voluntátis.
Laudámus te,
benedícimus te,
adorámus te,
glorificámus te,
grátias ágimus tibi propter magnam glóriam tuam.
Dómine Deus, Rex cæléstis,
Deus Pater omnípotens.

Dómine Fili unigénite, Jesu Christe,
Dómine Deus, Agnus Dei, Fílius Patris,
qui tollis peccáta mundi, miserére nobis;
qui tollis peccáta mundi,
   súscipe deprecatiónem nostram.
Qui sedes ad déxteram Patris, miserére nobis.

Quóniam tu solus Sanctus, tu solus Dóminus,
   tu solus Altissimus,
Jesu Christe, cum Sancto Spíritu: in glória Dei Patris.
Amen.

When this hymn is concluded, the Priest says:

Pr.   Let us pray.

And all pray in silence. Then the Priest says the Collect prayer, which ends:

R.   **Amen.**

The Liturgy of the Word

By hearing the word proclaimed in worship, the faithful again enter into a dialogue with God.

First Reading

The reader goes to the ambo and proclaims the First Reading, while all sit and listen. The reader ends:

> The word of the Lord.

R. **Thanks be to God.**

It is appropriate to have a brief time of quiet between readings as those present take the word of God to heart.

Psalm

The psalmist or cantor sings or says the Psalm, with the people making the response.

Second Reading

On Sundays and certain other days there is a second reading. It concludes with the same response as above.

Gospel

The assembly stands for the Gospel Acclamation. Except during Lent the Acclamation is:

R. **Alleluia.**

During Lent the following forms are used:

    R.   **Praise to you, O Christ, King of eternal glory!**
       Or:

    R.   **Praise and honour to you, Lord Jesus!**
       Or:

    R.   **Glory and praise to you, O Christ!**
       Or:

    R.   **Glory to you, O Christ,**
       you are the Word of God!

At the ambo the Deacon, or the Priest says:

    Pr.   The Lord be with you.

    R.   **And with your spirit.**

    Pr.   A reading from the holy Gospel according to N.

He makes the Sign of the Cross on the book and, together with the people, on his forehead, lips, and breast.

    R.   **Glory to you, O Lord.**

At the end of the Gospel:

    Pr.   The Gospel of the Lord.

    R.   **Praise to you, Lord Jesus Christ.**

After the Gospel all sit to listen to the Homily.

The Homily

Then follows the Homily, which is preached by a Priest or Deacon on all Sundays and Holydays of Obligation. After a brief silence all stand.

The Creed

On Sundays and Solemnities, the Profession of Faith will follow. The Apostles' Creed may be used.

The Niceno-Constantinopolitan Creed

I believe in one God,
the Father almighty,
maker of heaven and earth,
of all things visible and invisible.

I believe in one Lord Jesus Christ,
the Only Begotten Son of God,
born of the Father before all ages.
God from God, Light from Light,
true God from true God, begotten, not made,
consubstantial with the Father;
through him all things were made.
For us men and for our salvation
he came down from heaven, (*all bow*)
and by the Holy Spirit was incarnate
   of the Virgin Mary, and became man.

For our sake he was crucified under Pontius Pilate,
he suffered death and was buried
and rose again on the third day
in accordance with the Scriptures.
He ascended into heaven
and is seated at the right hand of the Father.
He will come again in glory
to judge the living and the dead
and his kingdom will have no end.

I believe in the Holy Spirit, the Lord, the giver of life,
who proceeds from the Father and the Son,
who with the Father and the Son
   is adored and glorified,
who has spoken through the prophets.

I believe in one, holy, catholic and apostolic Church.
I confess one Baptism for the forgiveness of sins
and I look forward to the resurrection of the dead
and the life of the world to come. Amen.

Credo in unum Deum,
Patrem omnipoténtem,
factórem cæli et terræ,
visibílium ómnium et invisibílium.

Et in unum Dóminum Jesum Christum,
Fílium Dei unigénitum,
et ex Patre natum ante ómnia sáecula.
Deum de Deo, lumen de lúmine,
    Deum verum de Deo vero,
génitum, non factum, consubstantiálem Patri:
per quem ómnia facta sunt.
Qui propter nos hómines et propter nostram salútem
descéndit de cælis. (*all bow*)
Et incarnátus est de Spiritu Sancto
    ex María Vírgine, et homo factus est.
Crucifíxus étiam pro nobis sub Póntio Piláto;
passus et sepúltus est,
et resurréxit tértia die, secúndum Scriptúras,
et ascéndit in cælum, sedet ad déxteram Patris.

Et íterum ventúrus est cum glória,
    iudicáre vivos et mórtuos,
cuius regni non erit finis.
Et in Spiritum Sanctum, Dóminum et vivificántem:
    qui ex Patre Filióque procédit.
Qui cum Patre et Fílio simul adorátur
    et conglorificátur:
qui locútus est per prophétas.

Et unam, sanctam, cathólicam
    et apostólicam Ecclésiam.
Confíteor unum baptísma in remissiónem peccatórum.
Et exspécto resurrectiónem mortuórum,
et vitam ventúri sáeculi.
Amen.

The Apostles' Creed

I believe in God,
the Father almighty,
Creator of heaven and earth,
and in Jesus Christ, his only Son, our Lord,
(*all bow*)
who was conceived by the Holy Spirit,
born of the Virgin Mary,
suffered under Pontius Pilate,
was crucified, died and was buried;
he descended into hell;
on the third day he rose again from the dead;
he ascended into heaven,
and is seated at the right hand of God
the Father almighty;
from there he will come to judge the living
and the dead.

I believe in the Holy Spirit,
the holy catholic Church,
the communion of saints,
the forgiveness of sins,
the resurrection of the body,
and life everlasting.
Amen.

Credo in Deum, Patrem omnipoténtem,
Creatórem caeli et terrae.
Et in Iesum Christum, Fílium eius únicum,
Dóminum nostrum:
(*all bow*)
qui concéptus est de Spíritu Sancto,
natus ex María Vírgine,
passus sub Póntio Piláto,
crucifíxus, mórtuus, et sepúltus;
descéndit ad inferos;
tértia die resurréxit a mórtuis;
ascéndit ad caelos;
sedet ad déxteram Dei Patris omnipoténtis;
inde ventúrus est iudicáre vivos et mórtuos.

Credo in Spíritum Sanctum,
sanctam Ecclésiam Cathólicam,
Sanctórum communiónem,
remissiónem peccatórum,
carnis resurrectiónem,
vitam aetérnam.
Amen.

The Prayer of the Faithful (Bidding Prayers)

Intentions will normally be for the Church; for the world; for those in particular need; and for the local community.

After each there is time for silent prayer, followed by the next intention, or concluded with a sung phrase such as

> **Christ, hear us,**
> *or* **Christ graciously hear us,**
> *or* *by a responsory such as:*
> Let us pray to the Lord.

R. **Grant this, almighty God.** *Or:*

R. **Lord, have mercy.** *Or:*

R. **Kyrie, eleison.**

The Priest concludes the Prayer with a collect.

The Liturgy of the Eucharist

For Catholics, the Eucharist is the source and summit of the whole Christian Life.

After the Liturgy of the Word, the people sit and the Offertory Chant begins. The faithful express their participation by making an offering, bringing forward bread and wine for the celebration of the Eucharist.

Preparatory Prayers

Standing at the altar, the Priest takes the paten with the bread and holds it slightly raised above the altar with both hands, saying:

Pr. Blessed are you, Lord God of all creation,
for through your goodness we have received
the bread we offer you:
fruit of the earth and work of human hands,
it will become for us the bread of life.

R. **Blessed be God for ever.**

The Priest then takes the chalice and holds it slightly raised above the altar with both hands, saying:

Pr. Blessed are you, Lord God of all creation,
for through your goodness we have received
the wine we offer you:
fruit of the vine and work of human hands,
it will become our spiritual drink.

R. **Blessed be God for ever.**

The Priest completes additional personal preparatory rites,
and the people rise as he says:

Pr. Pray, brethren (brothers and sisters),
that my sacrifice and yours
may be acceptable to God,
the almighty Father.

R. **May the Lord accept the sacrifice at your hands**
for the praise and glory of his name,
for our good
and the good of all his holy Church.

The Prayer over the Offerings

The Priest says the Prayer over the Offerings, at the end of
which the people acclaim:

R. **Amen.**

The Eucharistic Prayer

Extending his hands, the Priest says:

Pr. The Lord be with you.

R. **And with your spirit.**

Pr. Lift up your hearts.

R. **We lift them up to the Lord.**

Pr. Let us give thanks to the Lord our God.

R. **It is right and just.**

The Priest continues with the Preface appropriate to the season or feast at the end of which all sing or say:

Holy, Holy, Holy Lord God of hosts.
Heaven and earth are full of your glory.
Hosanna in the highest.
Blessed is he who comes in the name of the Lord.
Hosanna in the highest.

After the Sanctus the congregation kneels for the remainder of the Eucharistic Prayer.

Eucharistic Prayer I
(The Roman Canon)

Pr. To you, therefore, most merciful Father,
we make humble prayer and petition
through Jesus Christ, your Son, our Lord:
that you accept
and bless ✠ these gifts, these offerings,
these holy and unblemished sacrifices,
which we offer you firstly
for your holy catholic Church.
Be pleased to grant her peace,
to guard, unite and govern her
throughout the whole world,
together with your servant N. our Pope
and N. our Bishop,[8]
and all those who, holding to the truth,
hand on the catholic and apostolic faith.

Remember, Lord, your servants N. and N.
and all gathered here,
whose faith and devotion are known to you.
For them, we offer you this sacrifice of praise
or they offer it for themselves
and all who are dear to them:
for the redemption of their souls,
in hope of health and well-being,
and paying their homage to you,
the eternal God, living and true.

---

[8] Mention may be made here of the Coadjutor Bishop, or Auxiliary Bishops.

In communion with those whose memory we venerate,
especially the glorious ever-Virgin Mary,
Mother of our God and Lord, Jesus Christ,
† and blessed Joseph, her Spouse,
your blessed Apostles and Martyrs,
Peter and Paul, Andrew,
(James, John,
Thomas, James, Philip,
Bartholomew, Matthew,
Simon and Jude;
Linus, Cletus, Clement, Sixtus,
Cornelius, Cyprian,
Lawrence, Chrysogonus,
John and Paul,
Cosmas and Damian)
and all your Saints;
we ask that through their merits and prayers,
in all things we may be defended
by your protecting help.
(Through Christ our Lord. Amen.)

Therefore, Lord, we pray:
graciously accept this oblation of our service,
that of your whole family;
order our days in your peace,
and command that we be delivered
    from eternal damnation
and counted among the flock of those you have chosen.
(Through Christ our Lord. Amen.)

Be pleased, O God, we pray,
to bless, acknowledge,
and approve this offering in every respect;
make it spiritual and acceptable,
so that it may become for us
the Body and Blood of your most beloved Son,
our Lord Jesus Christ.

On the day before he was to suffer,
he took bread in his holy and venerable hands,
and with eyes raised to heaven
to you, O God, his almighty Father,
giving you thanks, he said the blessing,
broke the bread
and gave it to his disciples, saying:

TAKE THIS, ALL OF YOU, AND EAT OF IT,

FOR THIS IS MY BODY,

WHICH WILL BE GIVEN UP FOR YOU.

In a similar way, when supper was ended,
he took this precious chalice
in his holy and venerable hands,
and once more giving you thanks, he said the blessing
and gave the chalice to his disciples, saying:

TAKE THIS, ALL OF YOU, AND DRINK FROM IT,

FOR THIS IS THE CHALICE OF MY BLOOD,

THE BLOOD OF THE NEW AND ETERNAL COVENANT,

WHICH WILL BE POURED OUT FOR YOU AND FOR MANY

FOR THE FORGIVENESS OF SINS.

DO THIS IN MEMORY OF ME.

Pr.   The mystery of faith.

The people continue, acclaiming one of the following:

1.   **We proclaim your Death, O Lord,
      and profess your Resurrection
      until you come again.**

2.   **When we eat this Bread and drink this Cup,
      we proclaim your Death, O Lord,
      until you come again.**

3.   **Save us, Saviour of the world,
      for by your Cross and Resurrection
      you have set us free.**

Pr. Therefore, O Lord,
as we celebrate the memorial of the blessed Passion,
the Resurrection from the dead,
and the glorious Ascension into heaven
of Christ, your Son, our Lord,
we, your servants and your holy people,
offer to your glorious majesty
from the gifts that you have given us,
this pure victim,
this holy victim,
this spotless victim,
the holy Bread of eternal life
and the Chalice of everlasting salvation.

Be pleased to look upon these offerings
with a serene and kindly countenance,
and to accept them,
as once you were pleased to accept
the gifts of your servant Abel the just,
the sacrifice of Abraham, our father in faith,
and the offering of your high priest Melchizedek,
a holy sacrifice, a spotless victim.

In humble prayer we ask you, almighty God:
command that these gifts be borne
by the hands of your holy Angel
to your altar on high
in the sight of your divine majesty,
so that all of us, who through this participation
    at the altar
receive the most holy Body and Blood of your Son,
may be filled with every grace and heavenly blessing.
(Through Christ our Lord. Amen.)

Remember also, Lord, your servants N. and N.,
who have gone before us with the sign of faith
and rest in the sleep of peace.
Grant them, O Lord, we pray,
and all who sleep in Christ,
a place of refreshment, light and peace.
(Through Christ our Lord. Amen.)

To us, also, your servants, who, though sinners,
hope in your abundant mercies,
graciously grant some share
and fellowship with your holy Apostles and Martyrs:
with John the Baptist, Stephen,
Matthias, Barnabas,
(Ignatius, Alexander,
Marcellinus, Peter,
Felicity, Perpetua,
Agatha, Lucy,
Agnes, Cecilia, Anastasia)
and all your Saints;
admit us, we beseech you,
into their company,
not weighing our merits,
but granting us your pardon,
through Christ our Lord.

Through whom
you continue to make all these good things, O Lord;
you sanctify them, fill them with life,
bless them, and bestow them upon us.

The Priest takes the chalice and the paten with the host:

Pr. Through him, and with him, and in him,
O God, almighty Father,
in the unity of the Holy Spirit,
all glory and honour is yours,
for ever and ever.
R. Amen.

Eucharistic Prayer II

Pr.   The Lord be with you.

R.   **And with your spirit.**

Pr.   Lift up your hearts.

R.   **We lift them up to the Lord.**

Pr.   Let us give thanks to the Lord our God.

R.   **It is right and just.**

Pr. It is truly right and just, our duty and our salvation, always and everywhere to give you thanks,
   Father most holy,
through your beloved Son, Jesus Christ,
your Word through whom you made all things,
whom you sent as our Saviour and Redeemer,
incarnate by the Holy Spirit and born of the Virgin.

Fulfilling your will and gaining for you a holy people,
he stretched out his hands as he endured his Passion,
so as to break the bonds of death
   and manifest the resurrection.

   And so, with the Angels and all the Saints we declare your glory, as with one voice we acclaim:

The people sing or say aloud the Sanctus as on p. 101.

Pr. You are indeed Holy, O Lord,
the fount of all holiness.
Make holy, therefore, these gifts, we pray,
by sending down your Spirit upon them
like the dewfall,
so that they may become for us
the Body and ✠ Blood of our Lord Jesus Christ.

At the time he was betrayed
and entered willingly into his Passion,
he took bread and, giving thanks, broke it,
and gave it to his disciples, saying:

TAKE THIS, ALL OF YOU, AND EAT OF IT,

FOR THIS IS MY BODY,

WHICH WILL BE GIVEN UP FOR YOU.

In a similar way, when supper was ended,
he took the chalice
and, once more giving thanks,
he gave it to his disciples, saying:

TAKE THIS, ALL OF YOU, AND DRINK FROM IT,

FOR THIS IS THE CHALICE OF MY BLOOD,

THE BLOOD OF THE NEW AND ETERNAL COVENANT,

WHICH WILL BE POURED OUT FOR YOU AND FOR MANY

FOR THE FORGIVENESS OF SINS.

DO THIS IN MEMORY OF ME.

Pr. The mystery of faith.

The people continue with one of the acclamations on page 105.

Pr. Therefore, as we celebrate
the memorial of his Death and Resurrection,
we offer you, Lord,
the Bread of life and the Chalice of salvation,
giving thanks that you have held us worthy
to be in your presence and minister to you.

Humbly we pray
that, partaking of the Body and Blood of Christ,
we may be gathered into one by the Holy Spirit.

Remember, Lord, your Church,
spread throughout the world,
and bring her to the fullness of charity,
together with N. our Pope and N. our Bishop[9]
and all the clergy.

In Masses for the Dead, the following may be added:

Remember your servant N.,
whom you have called (today)
from this world to yourself.
Grant that he (she) who was united with your Son
    in a death like his,
may also be one with him in his Resurrection.

---

[9] Mention may be made here of the Coadjutor Bishop, or Auxiliary Bishops.

Remember also our brothers and sisters
who have fallen asleep in the hope of the resurrection,
and all who have died in your mercy:
welcome them into the light of your face.

Have mercy on us all,
we pray, that with the Blessed Virgin Mary,
	Mother of God,
with blessed Joseph, her Spouse,
with the blessed Apostles,
and all the Saints who have pleased you
	throughout the ages,
we may merit to be coheirs to eternal life,
and may praise and glorify you
through your Son, Jesus Christ.

The Priest takes the chalice and the paten with the host:

Through him, and with him, and in him,
O God, almighty Father,
in the unity of the Holy Spirit,
all glory and honour is yours,
for ever and ever.
R. Amen.

Eucharistic Prayer III

Pr. You are indeed Holy, O Lord,
and all you have created rightly gives you praise,
for through your Son our Lord Jesus Christ,
by the power and working of the Holy Spirit,
you give life to all things and make them holy,
and you never cease to gather a people to yourself,
so that from the rising of the sun to its setting
a pure sacrifice may be offered to your name.

Therefore, O Lord, we humbly implore you:
by the same Spirit graciously make holy
these gifts we have brought to you for consecration,
that they may become the Body and ✠ Blood
of your Son our Lord Jesus Christ,
at whose command we celebrate these mysteries.

For on the night he was betrayed
he himself took bread,
and, giving you thanks, he said the blessing,
broke the bread and gave it to his disciples, saying:

TAKE THIS, ALL OF YOU, AND EAT OF IT,

FOR THIS IS MY BODY,

WHICH WILL BE GIVEN UP FOR YOU.

In a similar way, when supper was ended,
he took the chalice,
and, giving you thanks, he said the blessing,
and gave the chalice to his disciples, saying:

TAKE THIS, ALL OF YOU, AND DRINK FROM IT,

FOR THIS IS THE CHALICE OF MY BLOOD

THE BLOOD OF THE NEW AND ETERNAL COVENANT,

WHICH WILL BE POURED OUT FOR YOU AND FOR MANY

FOR THE FORGIVENESS OF SINS.

DO THIS IN MEMORY OF ME.

Pr. The mystery of faith.

The people continue with one of the acclamations on page 105.

Pr. Therefore, O Lord, as we celebrate the memorial
of the saving Passion of your Son,
his wondrous Resurrection
and Ascension into heaven,
and as we look forward to his second coming,
we offer you in thanksgiving
this holy and living sacrifice.

Look, we pray, upon the oblation of your Church
and, recognising the sacrificial Victim by whose death
you willed to reconcile us to yourself,
grant that we, who are nourished
by the Body and Blood of your Son
and filled with his Holy Spirit,
may become one body, one spirit in Christ.

May he make of us
an eternal offering to you,
so that we may obtain an inheritance with your elect,
especially with the most Blessed Virgin Mary,
    Mother of God,
with blessed Joseph, her Spouse,
with your blessed Apostles and glorious Martyrs
(with Saint N.: *the Saint of the day or Patron Saint*)
and with all the Saints,
on whose constant intercession in your presence
we rely for unfailing help.

May this Sacrifice of our reconciliation,
we pray, O Lord,
advance the peace and salvation of all the world.
Be pleased to confirm in faith and charity
your pilgrim Church on earth,
with your servant N. our Pope and N. our Bishop,[10]
the Order of Bishops, all the clergy,
and the entire people you have gained for your own.

Listen graciously to the prayers of this family,
whom you have summoned before you:
in your compassion, O merciful Father,
gather to yourself all your children
scattered throughout the world.

† To our departed brothers and sisters
and to all who were pleasing to you
at their passing from this life,
give kind admittance to your kingdom.

There we hope to enjoy for ever the fullness
    of your glory
    through Christ our Lord,
through whom you bestow on the world all that is good.†

---

[10] Mention may be made here of the Coadjutor Bishop, or Auxiliary Bishops.

The Priest takes the chalice and the paten with the host:

Through him, and with him, and in him,
O God, almighty Father,
in the unity of the Holy Spirit,
all glory and honour is yours,
for ever and ever.
R. Amen.

Then follows the Communion Rite.

*When this Eucharistic Prayer is used in Masses for the Dead,
the following may be said:*

† Remember your servant N.
whom you have called (today)
from this world to yourself.
Grant that he (she) who was united with your Son
   in a death like his,
may also be one with him in his Resurrection,
when from the earth
he will raise up in the flesh those who have died,
and transform our lowly body
after the pattern of his own glorious body.
To our departed brothers and sisters, too,
and to all who were pleasing to you
at their passing from this life,
give kind admittance to your kingdom.
There we hope to enjoy for ever the fullness
   of your glory,
when you will wipe away every tear from our eyes.
For seeing you, our God, as you are,
we shall be like you for all the ages
and praise you without end,
(*He joins his hands*)
through Christ our Lord,
through whom you bestow on the world all that is good.†

Eucharistic Prayer IV

Pr. The Lord be with you.

R. And with your spirit.

Pr. Lift up your hearts.

R. We lift them up to the Lord.

Pr. Let us give thanks to the Lord our God.

R. It is right and just.

Pr. It is truly right to give you thanks,
truly just to give you glory, Father most holy,
for you are the one God living and true,
existing before all ages and abiding for all eternity,
dwelling in unapproachable light;
yet you, who alone are good, the source of life,
have made all that is,
so that you might fill your creatures with blessings
and bring joy to many of them by the glory of your light.

And so, in your presence are countless hosts of Angels,
who serve you day and night
and, gazing upon the glory of your face,
glorify you without ceasing.

With them we, too, confess your name in exultation,
giving voice to every creature under heaven,
as we acclaim:

The people sing or say aloud the Sanctus on page 101.

Pr. We give you praise, Father most holy,
for you are great
and you have fashioned all your works
in wisdom and in love.
You formed man in your own image
and entrusted the whole world to his care,
so that in serving you alone, the Creator,
he might have dominion over all creatures.
And when through disobedience
    he had lost your friendship,
you did not abandon him to the domain of death.
For you came in mercy to the aid of all,
so that those who seek might find you.
Time and again you offered them covenants
and through the prophets
taught them to look forward to salvation.

And you so loved the world, Father most holy,
that in the fullness of time
you sent your Only Begotten Son to be our Saviour.

Made incarnate by the Holy Spirit
and born of the Virgin Mary,
he shared our human nature in all things but sin.
To the poor he proclaimed the good news of salvation,
to prisoners, freedom,
and to the sorrowful of heart, joy.
To accomplish your plan,
he gave himself up to death,
and, rising from the dead,
he destroyed death and restored life.

And that we might live no longer for ourselves
but for him who died and rose again for us,
he sent the Holy Spirit from you, Father,
as the first fruits for those who believe,
so that, bringing to perfection his work in the world,
he might sanctify creation to the full.

Therefore, O Lord, we pray:
may this same Holy Spirit
graciously sanctify these offerings,
that they may become
the Body and ✠ Blood of our Lord Jesus Christ for the
celebration of this great mystery,
which he himself left us as an eternal covenant.

For when the hour had come
for him to be glorified by you, Father most holy,
having loved his own who were in the world,
he loved them to the end:
and while they were at supper, he took bread, blessed
and broke it, and gave it to his disciples, saying:

TAKE THIS, ALL OF YOU,

AND EAT OF IT,

FOR THIS IS MY BODY,

WHICH WILL BE GIVEN UP FOR YOU.

In a similar way, taking the chalice filled with the fruit
of the vine, he gave thanks, and gave the chalice to his
disciples, saying:

TAKE THIS, ALL OF YOU, AND DRINK FROM IT,

FOR THIS IS THE CHALICE OF MY BLOOD,

THE BLOOD OF THE NEW AND ETERNAL COVENANT,

WHICH WILL BE POURED OUT FOR YOU AND FOR MANY

FOR THE FORGIVENESS OF SINS.

DO THIS IN MEMORY OF ME.

Pr. The mystery of faith.

The people continue with one of the acclamations on page 105.

Pr. Therefore, O Lord,
as we now celebrate the memorial of our redemption,
we remember Christ's Death
and his descent to the realm of the dead,
we proclaim his Resurrection
and his Ascension to your right hand,
and, as we await his coming in glory,
we offer you his Body and Blood,
the sacrifice acceptable to you
which brings salvation to the whole world.

Look, O Lord, upon the Sacrifice
which you yourself have provided for your Church, and
grant in your loving kindness
to all who partake of this one Bread and one Chalice
that, gathered into one body by the Holy Spirit,
they may truly become a living sacrifice in Christ
to the praise of your glory.

Therefore, Lord, remember now
all for whom we offer this sacrifice:
especially your servant N. our Pope, N. our Bishop,[11]
and the whole Order of Bishops,
all the clergy,
those who take part in this offering,
those gathered here before you,
your entire people,
and all who seek you with a sincere heart.

Remember also
those who have died in the peace of your Christ
and all the dead,
whose faith you alone have known.

---

[11] Mention may be made here of the Coadjutor Bishop, or Auxiliary Bishops.

To all of us, your children,
grant, O merciful Father,
that we may enter into a heavenly inheritance
with the Blessed Virgin Mary, Mother of God,
with blessed Joseph, her Spouse,
and with your Apostles and Saints in your kingdom.
There, with the whole of creation,
freed from the corruption of sin and death,
may we glorify you through Christ our Lord,
through whom you bestow on the world all that is good.

The Priest takes the chalice and the paten with the host:

Through him, and with him, and in him,
O God, almighty Father,
in the unity of the Holy Spirit,
all glory and honour is yours,
for ever and ever.
R. Amen.

The Communion Rite

Eating and drinking together the Lord's Body and Blood in a paschal meal is the culmination of the Eucharist.

The Lord's Prayer

After the chalice and paten have been set down,
the congregation stands and the Priest says:

Pr. At the Saviour's command
and formed by divine teaching,
we dare to say:

Pr. Præceptis salutáribus móniti,
et divína institutióne formati,
audémus dicere:

Together with the people, he continues:

Our Father, who art in heaven,
hallowed be thy name;
thy kingdom come,
thy will be done on earth as it is in heaven.
Give us this day our daily bread,
and forgive us our trespasses,
as we forgive those who trespass against us;
and lead us not into temptation,
but deliver us from evil.

Pater noster, qui es in cælis;
sanctificétur nomen tuum;
advéniat regnum tuum;
fiat voluntas tua sicut in cælo, et in terra.
Panem nostrum cotidiánum da nobis hódie;
et dimítte nobis débita nostra,
sicut et nos dimíttimus debitóribus nostris;
et ne nos indúcas in tentatiónem;
sed líbera nos a malo.

Pr. Deliver us, Lord, we pray, from every evil,
graciously grant peace in our days,
that, by the help of your mercy,
we may be always free from sin
and safe from all distress,
as we await the blessed hope
and the coming of our Saviour, Jesus Christ.

**R. For the kingdom,
the power and the glory are yours
now and for ever.**

The Peace

Pr. Lord Jesus Christ,
who said to your Apostles:
Peace I leave you, my peace I give you;
look not on our sins,
but on the faith of your Church,
and graciously grant her peace and unity
in accordance with your will.
Who live and reign for ever and ever.
R. Amen.

Pr. The peace of the Lord be with you always.

R. And with your spirit.

Then the Deacon, or the Priest, adds:

Pr. Let us offer each other the sign of peace.

And all offer one another the customary sign of peace.

Breaking of the Bread

Then the Priest takes the host, breaks it over the paten, and places a small piece in the chalice, saying quietly:

Pr. May this mingling of the Body and Blood
of our Lord Jesus Christ bring eternal life
to us who receive it.

Meanwhile the following is sung or said:

> **Lamb of God, you take away the sins of the world,
> have mercy on us.**
>
> **Lamb of God, you take away the sins of the world,
> have mercy on us.**
>
> **Lamb of God, you take away the sins of the world,
> grant us peace.**

> **Agnus Dei, qui tollis peccáta mundi: miserére nobis.**
>
> **Agnus Dei, qui tollis peccáta mundi: miserére nobis.**
>
> **Agnus Dei, qui tollis peccáta mundi:
> dona nobis pacem.**

Invitation to Communion

All kneel. The Priest genuflects, takes the host and, holding it slightly raised above the paten or above the chalice says aloud:

> **Pr.** Behold the Lamb of God,
> behold him who takes away the sins of the world.
> Blessed are those called to the supper
> of the Lamb.
>
> **R.** **Lord, I am not worthy
> that you should enter under my roof,
> but only say the word
> and my soul shall be healed.**

While the Priest is receiving the Body of Christ, the Communion Chant begins.

Communion Procession

After the Priest has reverently consumed the Body and Blood of Christ he takes the paten or ciborium and approaches the communicants.

The Priest raises a host slightly and shows it to each of the communicants, saying:

Pr. The Body of Christ.

R. Amen.

When Communion is ministered from the chalice:

Pr. The Blood of Christ.

R. Amen.

After the distribution of Communion, if appropriate, a sacred silence may be observed for a while, or a psalm or other canticle of praise or a hymn may be sung. Then, the Priest says:

Pr. Let us pray.

Prayer after Communion

All stand and pray in silence for a while, unless silence has just been observed. Then the Priest says the Prayer after Communion, at the end of which the people acclaim:

R. Amen.

The Concluding Rites

The Mass closes, sending the faithful forth to put what they have celebrated into effect in their daily lives.

Any brief announcements follow here.

Then the Dismissal takes place.

Pr. The Lord be with you.

R. And with your spirit.

The Priest blesses the people, saying:

Pr. May almighty God bless you,
the Father, and the Son, ✠ and the Holy Spirit.

R. Amen.

Then the Deacon, or the Priest himself says the Dismissal:

Pr. Go forth, the Mass is ended.

R. Thanks be to God. *Or:*

Pr. Go and announce the Gospel of the Lord.

R. Thanks be to God. *Or:*

Pr. Go in peace, glorifying the Lord by your life.

R. Thanks be to God. *Or:*

Pr. Go in peace.

R. Thanks be to God.

Then the Priest venerates the altar as at the beginning.

*After making a profound bow with the ministers,
he withdraws.*

IF YOU CAN'T
GET TO MASS

Spiritual Communion

Spiritual Communion is the heartfelt desire to receive Our Lord, even when we are unable because of the distance or for some other reason. This desire to receive him through spiritual Communion is an act of love which prolongs our thanksgiving even when we are not in the Eucharistic presence of Our Lord. The wish to live constantly in his presence can be fuelled by acts of love and desire to be united with him and is a means of drawing more deeply from the life of the Holy Spirit dwelling within our souls in the state of grace. "The effects of a sacrament can be received by desire. Although in such a case the sacrament is not received physically…nevertheless the actual reception of the sacrament itself brings with it fuller effect than receiving it through desire alone" (*St Thomas Aquinas*). The writings of the saints reveal many formulae for making a spiritual Communion:

Acts of Spiritual Communion

My Jesus, I believe that you are truly present
in the Most Holy Sacrament.
I love you above all things,
and I desire to receive you into my soul.
Since I cannot at this moment
    receive you sacramentally,
come at least spiritually into my heart.
I embrace you as being already there
    and unite myself wholly to you.
Never permit me to be separated from you.
Amen.

(St Alphonsus Liguori)

I wish, my Lord, to receive you with the purity,
humility and devotion with which your
Most Holy Mother received you,
with the spirit and fervour of the saints.

Give me, good Lord,
a longing to be with you…
give me warmth, delight and quickness
    in thinking upon you.
And give me your grace to long
    for your holy sacraments,
and specially to rejoice in the presence
    of your very blessed Body,
sweet Saviour Christ,
in the Holy Sacrament of the altar.

(St Thomas More)

PRAYERS FOR HOLY
COMMUNION

Say these prayers slowly, a few words at a time. It is well to stop after every few words, that they may sink into the heart. Each prayer may be said several times.

Prayer before Mass

O God, to whom every heart is open,
every desire known and from whom
no secrets are hidden;
purify the thoughts of our hearts
    by the inspiration of your Holy Spirit,
that we may perfectly love you,
and worthily praise your holy name.
Amen.

Before Holy Communion

Prayer for Help

O God, help me to make a good Communion.
Mary, my dearest mother,
pray to Jesus for me.
My dear Angel Guardian,
lead me to the Altar of God.

Act of Faith

O God, because you have said it,
I believe that I shall receive
the Sacred Body of Jesus Christ to eat,
and his Precious Blood to drink.
My God, I believe this with all my heart.

Act of Humility

My God, I confess that I am a poor sinner;
I am not worthy to receive
the Body and Blood of Jesus,
   on account of my sins.
Lord, I am not worthy to receive you under my roof;
but only say the word, and my soul will be healed.

Act of Sorrow

My God, I detest all the sins of my life.
I am sorry for them,
because they have offended you, my God,
you who are so good.
I resolve never to commit sin any more.
My good God, pity me, have mercy on me, forgive me.

Act of Adoration

O Jesus, great God, present on the Altar,
I bow down before you.
I adore you.

Act of Love and Desire

Jesus, I love you.
I desire with all my heart to receive you.
Jesus, come into my poor soul,
and give me your Flesh to eat and your Blood to drink.
Give me your whole Self, Body, Blood, Soul and Divinity,
that I may live for ever with you.

Prayer of St Thomas Aquinas

Almighty and ever-living God,
I approach the sacrament
of your only-begotten Son,
our Lord Jesus Christ.
I come sick to the doctor of life,
unclean to the fountain of mercy,
blind to the radiance of eternal light,
poor and needy to the Lord of heaven and earth.
Lord in your great generosity, heal my sickness,
wash away my defilement, enlighten my blindness,
enrich my poverty, and clothe my nakedness.

May I receive the bread of angels,
the King of kings and Lord of lords,
with humble reverence, with purity and faith,
with repentance and love and the determined purpose
that will help to bring me to salvation.
May I receive the sacrament of the Lord's body
and blood and its reality and power.

Kind God, may I receive the body
of your only begotten Son, our Lord Jesus Christ,
born from the womb of the Virgin Mary,
and so be received into his mystical body
and numbered among his members.
Loving Father, as on my earthly pilgrimage
I now receive your beloved Son under the veil
of a sacrament,
may I one day see him face to face in glory,
who lives and reigns with you for ever.
Amen.

Receiving Holy Communion

When the priest or minister says "The Body of Christ", answer "Amen" and receive the sacred host with reverence. If you receive Holy Communion in the hand, place the host reverently into your mouth before returning to your place. If Holy Communion is given from the chalice, answer "Amen" when the priest or minister says "The Blood of Christ"; take the chalice and drink a little of the Precious Blood, taking care not to spill any. Say in your heart, with all the faith of St Thomas "My Lord and my God". Jesus is now really present in you. Keep away all earthly thoughts and enjoy his presence.

After Holy Communion

I give you thanks

I give you thanks, Lord, Holy Father, everlasting God.
In your great mercy,
and not because of my own merits,
you have fed me a sinner and your unworthy servant,
with the precious body and blood of your Son,
our Lord Jesus Christ.
I pray that this Holy Communion may not serve
    as my judgement and condemnation,
but as my forgiveness and salvation.
May it be my armour of faith and shield of good purpose,
root out in me all that is evil and increase every virtue.
I beseech you to bring me a sinner,
to that great feast where,
with your Son and the Holy Spirit you are the true light
    of your holy ones,
their flawless blessedness,
everlasting joy and perfect happiness.
Through Christ our Lord.
Amen.

(St Thomas Aquinas)

Act of Faith

O Jesus, I believe that I have received your Flesh
to eat and your Blood to drink,
because you have said it,
and your word is true.
All that I have and all that I am are your gift
    and now you have given me yourself.

Act of Adoration

O Jesus, my God, my Creator, I adore you,
because from your hands I came and with you
I am to be happy for ever.

Act of Humility

O Jesus, I am not worthy to receive you,
and yet you have come to me that my poor heart
may learn of you to be meek and humble.

Act of Love

Jesus, I love you;
I love you with all my heart.
You know that I love you,
and wish to love you daily more and more.

Act of Thanksgiving

My good Jesus, I thank you with all my heart.
How good, how kind you are to me.
Blessed be Jesus
    in the most holy Sacrament of the Altar.

Act of Offering

O Jesus, receive my poor offering. Jesus, you have given yourself to me, and now let me give myself to you: I give you my body, that I may be chaste and pure. I give you my soul, that I may be free from sin. I give you my heart, that I may always love you. I give you my every breath that I shall breathe, and especially my last. I give you myself in life and in death, that I may be yours for ever and ever.

For Yourself

O Jesus, wash away my sins
with your Precious Blood.
O Jesus, the struggle against temptation
   is not yet finished.
My Jesus, when temptation comes near me,
make me strong against it.
In the moment of temptation may I always say:
"My Jesus, mercy! Mary, help!"
O Jesus, may I lead a good life;
may I die a happy death.
May I receive you before I die.
May I say when I am dying:
"Jesus, Mary and Joseph, I give you my heart and my soul".

Listen now for a moment to Jesus Christ; perhaps he has something to say to you. Answer Jesus in your heart, and tell him all your troubles. Then say:

For Perseverance

J esus, I am going away for a time,
but I trust not without you.
You are with me by your grace.
I resolve never to leave you by mortal sin.
Although I am so weak I have such hope in you.
Give me grace to persevere. Amen.

A VISIT TO
THE BLESSED
SACRAMENT

Sitting or kneeling before Jesus truly present in the Blessed Sacrament, it may be helpful to reflect on the love and tenderness of our Lord, by meditating upon this (or another) passage of Scripture:

"No one can come to me unless he is drawn by the Father who sent me, and I will raise him up at the last day. It is written in the prophets: They will all be taught by God, and to hear the teaching of the Father, and learn from it, is to come to me. Not that anybody has seen the Father, except the one who comes from God: he has seen the Father. I tell you most solemnly, everybody who believes has eternal life. I am the bread of life. Your fathers ate the manna in the desert and they are dead; but this is the bread that comes down from heaven, so that a man may eat it and not die. I am the living bread which has come down from heaven.

"Anyone who eats this bread will live for ever; and the bread that I shall give is my flesh, for the life of the world." Then the Jews started arguing with one another: "How can this man give us his flesh to eat?" they said. Jesus replied: "I tell you most solemnly, if you do not eat the flesh of the Son of Man and drink his blood, you will not have life in you. Anyone who does eat my flesh and drink my blood has eternal life, and I shall raise him up on the last day.

"For my flesh is real food and my blood is real drink. He who eats my flesh and drinks my blood lives in me and I live in him. As I, who am sent by the living Father, myself draw life from the Father, so whoever eats me will draw life from me.

"This is the bread come down from heaven; not like the bread our ancestors ate: they are dead, but anyone who eats this bread will live for ever."

He taught this doctrine at Capernaum, in the synagogue. After hearing it, many of his followers said, "This is intolerable language. How could anyone accept it?" Jesus was aware that his followers were complaining about it and said, "Does this upset you? What if you should see the Son of Man ascend to where he was before? 'It is the spirit that gives life, the flesh has nothing to offer. The words I have spoken to you are spirit and they are life.' But there are some of you who do not believe."

For Jesus knew from the outset those who did not believe, and who it was that would betray him. He went on, "This is why I told you that no one could come to me unless the Father allows him". After this, many of his disciples left him and stopped going with him. Then Jesus said to the Twelve, "What about you, do you want to go away too?" Simon Peter answered, "Lord, who shall we go to? You have the message of eternal life, and we believe; we know that you are the Holy One of God."

(John 6:44-69)

THE SECRET
OF JOY

The Secret of Joy

The joy that we search for is not grounded primarily in material things, success and the pleasures of this world, because its source is somewhere else. This joy is not psychological but spiritual: it is in God himself.

All the saints, without exception, shone with an ineffable and unshakable joy, even in their worst sufferings. Why?

Why did they glow with this inexpressible joy that often made their enemies jealous, when they lacked everything in the world's eyes and were more often than not humiliated, poor or ill?

It is because their joy was not founded on success, health or honours. Their joy was in God and indeed was God himself. We too can and should discover their secret.

Joy is a Gift

Nobody can acquire joy by him or herself, because it is a free gift from God. We will see later how it is our responsibility to make it grow and to nurture it so that it doesn't die, but we must not forget that it is above all a gift. It is one of those paradoxes: it is both within and outside us, as it is a gift from God.

So we should not seek it for itself or for our own well-being and personal satisfaction. That would imply that we seek God for the delight that his presence gives our souls rather than for himself.

But if we receive joy as a present from God, we resemble the man who has discovered a pearl in a field and who sells everything he owns to "buy" that field (cf. *Matthew* 13:45).

Joy is that precious pearl, most often deposited in the field of our hearts and that God has freely given to us.

Perhaps we have discovered it without great exertion, because he has come to us and deposited that treasure in our hearts. But he expects us to do everything in our power to guard that treasure in order that the wealth of joy that has accumulated in us does not dissipate.

This kind of joy does not wear off or wither like the fleeting joys that the world can bring. But it is up to us whether we make it grow or leave it deeply buried without bearing fruit.

Joy and Conversion

Welcoming God's joy will always involve an increasing conversion on our part, and an examination of anything that could sully and smother this joy. Its birth goes hand in hand with an inner purification that cuts away the vain desires of our hearts and all those masks that we have created in order not to see ourselves poor and naked as we really are.

Joy is born of truth. People have kept in the depths of their hearts a taste for joy born of truth. But at the same time, it makes them scared because they sense that if they open themselves to this joy and truth, it will throw back at them the true image of themselves, bared of all artifice and make-up.

Neither can joy be experienced without our being humbled, whatever form that humbling and death to ourselves will take. By discovering our weaknesses, God will show us a very particular joy: that of knowing and feeling that despite them, and even because of them, he loves us no less.

This discovery is at the heart of the spirituality of Thérèse of Lisieux, the saint who found her joy in her weaknesses; not because of them but because of the goodness and tenderness of God towards her.

What a sweet joy to think that the Good God is just, that he takes our weaknesses into account and that he knows perfectly the fragility of our nature.

(St Thérèse of Lisieux)

This confidence in the tenderness of the Father gives to Thérèsian joy a note of peace, which is its principal characteristic. She knows she is poor and she feels weak, but she does not try to mark her own weaknesses. On the contrary, she finds her joy in admitting her littleness.

So we have to be small in order to taste true joy deeply. If we, from our high positions, refuse to humble ourselves, we will never know joy. On the contrary we will always need more sadness to feed our own revolt against God, against others...and against ourselves as well.

There is much humility in accepting happiness, and pride needs unhappiness to feed its revolt.

(Cardinal Danielou)

So let us accept the conversion of heart that God implores of us: let us go back to him as to a Father, and he will overcome us with his joy. Repentance itself often provokes in us a certain joy, sometimes mixed with tears. It is joy nonetheless because we understand from within that God would not reduce us to the faults we have committed. God's tenderness softens our hearts, and the tears that come with admitting our sin are the sign of a healthy surrender of a heart that renounces its self-sufficiency and opens itself to God's mercy.

The Father's joy welcomes the prodigal son and tells his returning child of his own joy:

There will be more rejoicing in heaven over one repentant sinner than over ninety-nine virtuous men who have no need of repentance.

(Luke 15:7)

Joy is Inner Freedom

In general terms, conversion is a starting point towards a more intense discover of real joy. But in order to discover this, we have to accept to undergo an inner development in which our hearts will let themselves be rained and rid of their false joys.

Covetousness corrupts, and can even corrupt the blessings offered by God. The risk, especially at the beginnings of a spiritual life, is to accept the gifts of God without wanting to go to their source. The Lord will progressively train our desires in order to make us grow in the inner freedom that is so necessary to taste joy.

The path towards a free heart is often steep and at times hard. Perhaps we will have to bear some tiresome struggles and renounce many passing pleasures, to taste a little of this inner freedom. But if we toil for it, we know that the joy that results will be worth the effort; for the joy that God gives us to taste is not comparable to the joys of a heart that lets itself be led according to its instincts and desires.

It would be wrong to think that inner freedom is achieved within a kind of rigidity, or stoicism, in order to no longer feel or experience anything. A free soul continues to feel its littleness and poverty, but it is so strongly anchored in God that it does not fear anything. Instead of being obstacles to inner freedom, its weaknesses are real springboards to greater holiness.

A free soul that lives in peace and joy has no need of other people to fill its inner emptiness or to entertain it. That soul loves other people for who they are and not for the well-being that they might bring to it.

Our God is a God of Joy

Christianity is joy, mainly because it enables Christians to enter into the joy of the Trinity. Joy is the sort of climate that reigns in God. We are used to saying that God is Mercy, Peace, Joy, etc.

As Father François Varillon has observed, we would have to say that God is only Love, in order for us to approach the mystery of God in the right way. It is this Love that is good, merciful, joyful, etc.

In whatever circumstance we live, we are able to learn by heart the divine attributes that have been revealed to us. For example, we may experience God's fatherly goodness in our own needs, or Jesus's mercy in forgiving our sins.

To taste joy, we actually have to take the plunge in what is the Trinitarian climate. God the Father, God the Son and God the Holy Spirit live together in perfect and total joy because of their love for one another.

The fulness of God's joy comes from the mutual gift of the Persons of the Trinity. In fact as soon as something is given, there is potential joy. This gift is complete in God, and so his joy is full… The Father gives the Son joy by giving himself totally to him. The Son provides his Father joy by surrendering himself totally too. Each is the Other's joy. And to give an image of this, we could say that this "explosion of joy" between them is a Person: the Holy Spirit.

The Holy Spirit, Teacher of Divine Joy

Our imitation of the joy that exists in God is supposed to be very brief. Yet we have just noticed that the Holy Spirit is maybe the divine Person who can best teach us what real joy is. The New Testament is full of references of this kind:

What the Spirit brings is… love, joy, peace. (Galatians 5:22)

The disciples were filled with joy and the Holy Spirit. (Acts 13:52)

It would take too long to list all the quotations in which joy is directly linked to the Person of the Holy Spirit. However, it is to him that our need to learn real joy should be addressed. Jesus and Mary were filled with joy by him (cf. *Luke* 10:21).

When he ascended to the Father, Jesus promised his disciples (and so to the nascent Church) that he would not leave them orphaned. He promised them the gift of his Spirit so that he might introduce them himself to the joy of "possessing God".

The joy that comes to the Church from the Holy Spirit is a bride's joy: the Church is Christ's Bride. We who are her sons and daughters have a share in that heritage if we open ourselves to it.

One small detail that is no less significant is that, on the eve of Pentecost in 1975, Paul VI published his Encyclical on joy *Gaudete in Domino*. He wanted to show Christians how the gifts of the Spirit could teach them to welcome true joy.

Love and Joy in God

We have seen together that joy in God comes from the gift that each Person of the Trinity makes of himself. It is not our concern here to give thorough theological proof for the links between joy and love. Nevertheless, our hearts can easily make out that this gift is a gift of love. It is because of the ineffable love with which he knew the Father loved him that Jesus shone forth with such joy and peace.

When we give of ourselves, it can only be in a spirit of love, or else we are not truly giving ourselves. Conversely, the person who loves can only give of him or herself, or else they are not truly loving.

The world has seen and continues to see in God, a kind of tyrant who is ceaselessly on the look-out for the weakness and sin of mankind. He appears to the world as a distant being, indifferent to what is lived here on earth. If such are the images that the world has of God, it is not surprising that it does not want to come near to him. How could we believe in the love of such a God? How could we want to love him in return and believe that he can give us his joy?

And yet God is love and the source of all joy. All those who experience a real encounter with the Loving God and who - in one way or another - follow him, can take part in his joy:

I have made your name known to them
And will continue to make it known,
So that the love with which you loved me may be in them,
And so that I may be in them. (John 17:26)

To know that we are loved and chosen by God as his children: is that not a profound joy? To rejoice in God with his very joy: is that not, after all, our vocation as Christians?

God did not want to keep his joy to himself. By creating the universe and by forming man in his image and likeness, he wanted to share his joy with us. He did not create man for his own beatitude because he "suffices" for himself. In this sense, we don't add anything to his joy. He created us out of an overflowing love, to give himself to us and to communicate his own joy to us.

Communion and Contemplation

Having been created in the image and likeness of God, we are made for joy, although only insofar as we enter in communion with our Creator.

One of the greatest obstacles to Christian joy lies in an abandonment of contemplation, because it is contemplation that introduces us to the presence and the source of our joy: God himself. Moreover, by prayer and contemplation, the Lord lets himself be touched and seized by the soul that loves him. In this way, he tells him what he is: goodness, gentleness, peace, love, joy, etc.

Generally speaking in fact, joy is born of the very close presence of that which we love. All the more reason for real and profound joy to come from the presence, close to and within us, of he whom we love.

A Christian can lack everything, but if he is united to God in faith and charity, he will not lack joy.

(Paul VI)

In his Encyclical, Paul VI also reminded us that people find joy "in possessing something known and loved."

Through contemplation, God gives himself to man. We find inexpressible joy in this.

This requires from us a certain faithfulness in the practice of prayer, so that we can surpass the obstacles of aridity and hardness inherent to every person's prayer life. Insofar as we persevere, God will not fail to shed in our hearts a certain gentle sweetness that will speak of his presence.

Contemplation is the beginning of joy that will have no end.
(Father Thomas Dehaut)

We are told that the angels, who perpetually contemplate the face of God, are forever rejoicing. God cannot deprive us of such a joy if we stand in his presence in contemplation: *I will make them joyful in my house of prayer (Isaiah 56:6).*

In this way, we will be able to taste truly spiritual joy: our hearts will find their ultimate rest and joy in possessing God who will give himself over to us. Let us make equally clear that this experience of God's presence does not bring a superficial joy, like a boisterous cheerfulness, or a smug passivity. It brings instead a profound joy that nothing can spoil.

The more a soul enters into communion with God, the more it is united to him; and the more it finds its joy in discovering that everything it experiences has a meaning. It discovers God everywhere, it understands the reason for its existence. The mysteries of the kingdom of God disclose themselves to it gradually, and thus it can marvel that the whole economy of salvation is ordered around the sole presence of Jesus who reveals himself to it.

Christ is the joy of life! He is joy because he gives our life its true meaning, dignity and security.

(Paul VI)

Joy and the Gift of Ourselves

This joy that is born of communion with God cannot dwell in us without having any effect on us. It will provoke us to give of ourselves. It will always invite us to go further and surpass our own limits so that we can give of ourselves more completely and gratuitously. Thanks to this, the joy will grow and bear fruit. It is an immense joy to give of oneself: to God and then others, as if through an outpouring:

There is more happiness in giving than in receiving

(Acts 20:35)

One of the biggest obstacles to the blossoming of joy is withdrawing into oneself. Generally, we turn in on ourselves in areas that hurt us or out of fear that we will not be able to fulfil our needs.

There are moments - or spheres - in which we feel incapable of giving of ourselves. But perhaps God asks us, in the first instance, to give of ourselves where we are able to. Little by little, he will take care of reducing our inner limits himself, insofar as we allow him. Perhaps this will happen at the cost of certain agonising struggles, but it will always be for our greater joy and his.

In order not to expose ourselves to the sadness that withdrawing into ourselves provokes, we need to ask the Lord for the grace definitively to renounce any such withdrawal that is deliberate. I know some people who have made this "gamble", confiding themselves to God's grace, and he responded. They themselves have said that even with struggles at certain moments, this promise to the Lord made them grow more quickly in joy than they could have foreseen.

PRAYERS TO THE
HOLY SPIRIT

The Fruits of the Holy Spirit
A Novena

Day One - Love

Hymn (*See pp.187-190*)

Antiphon

Come, Holy Spirit, fill the hearts of your faithful, and kindle in them the fire of your love.
Send forth your Spirit,
and they will be created,
- And you will renew the face of the earth.

Prayer

God our Father,
your love for us gives us strength to accomplish your will.
Fill us, as you filled St Philip,
with the love of your Holy Spirit,
so that like him we may share your love with others.
We ask this through Christ our Lord.
Amen.

Reading
(*1 John 4:7-9*)

Beloved, let us love one another, because love is of God; everyone who loves is begotten by God and knows God. Whoever is without love does not know God, for God is love. In this way the love of God was revealed to us: God sent his only Son into the world so that we might have life through him.

Responsory

(cf. Romans 5:5; 8:11)

The love of God has been poured into our hearts (alleluia).

By his Spirit living in us (alleluia).

Meditation

I love, and loving must love ceaselessly, So whole a conquest in me love hath won; My love to Thee, Thy love to me dost run; In Thee I live, and Thou dost live in me.

These words, from one of the two sonnets that survive from St Philip, summarise well the way that he experienced and understood the love of God and neighbour. "We must give ourselves to God altogether," he insisted, for God has already given himself completely to us. As St Thomas says, in the fruit of love "the Holy Spirit is given in a special manner, as in his own likeness, since he himself is love." Such a total gift of self on God's part demands a response that is likewise total, and leaves no room for any rival. "As much love as we give to creatures," St Philip says, "just so much do we take from the Creator."

Yet he will insist over and over that the fruit of our love for God must be visible in the love we have for our neighbours, and in our concern for them in their need: "God never comes where there is no love of neighbour." From the very beginning of his days in Rome, long before his ordination as a priest, and even before his Pentecost, St Philip organised charitable groups and institutions in the city. Later, during the Holy Year of 1550, he established the Confraternity of the Holy Trinity (*Santissima Trinità dei Pellegrini*) to serve the pilgrims who came to Rome for the Jubilee. This work continued in subsequent Holy Years, and in the interim the confraternity devoted itself to caring for the sick in hospitals and convalescent homes.

St Philip frequently joined in their work, even in his old age, and constantly sent his penitents to the hospitals as well. "A diligent charity in ministering to the sick," he advised them, "is a compendious way to the acquisition of perfect virtue." This was dirty, exhausting, thankless work, but he performed it with cheerfulness and an evident love - and expected his disciples to come to it with the same attitude. Many found it a great mortification, especially those who in their own lives were used to being cared for and waited on, rather than the other way around. But this mortification of self-will and pride is at the heart of St Philip's spiritual approach, and was for him the measure of all spiritual progress:

"The greatness of our love for God must be tested by the desire we have of suffering for his love." He was not oblivious to the sacrifices that works of charity involved, but he knew that real charity would overcome these obstacles. "The love of God makes us do great things."

Litany (Optional; see p.191)
Our Father, Hail Mary, Glory be.

Concluding prayer

Heavenly Father, hear the prayers that we make in the name of your Son,
and give us the Paraclete whom he promised
    you would send.
May your love for us give us strength
    to respond to you,
and to bear fruit in our love for you
    and for our neighbour.
We ask this through Christ our Lord. Amen.

Day Two - Joy

Hymn *(See pp.187-190)*

Antiphon

Come, Holy Spirit, fill the hearts of your faithful, and kindle in them the fire of your love.
Send forth your Spirit,
and they will be created,
- And you will renew the face of the earth.

Prayer

Father, the presence of your Holy Spirit gives joy to your people.
Open our hearts to receive your Spirit,
that like St Philip we may rejoice in his presence
every day of our lives.
We ask this through Christ our Lord.
Amen.

Reading

(1 Peter 1:8-9)

Although you have never seen [Christ] you love him; even though you do not see him now you believe in him, you rejoice with an indescribable and glorious joy, as you attain the goal of your faith, the salvation of your souls.

Responsory

(cf. Romans 5:5; 8:11)

The love of God has been poured into our hearts (alleluia).

- By his Spirit living in us (alleluia).

Meditation

"The necessary result of the love of charity is joy: because every lover rejoices at being united to the beloved." So teaches St Thomas, and this fruit of the Spirit was so evident in the life of St Philip that it has become almost synonymous with his name. "Light of Holy Joy" Cardinal Newman calls him, and a contemporary author who wrote a philosophical treatise on the subject titled his work simply "Philip: Or Christian Joy". Many eyewitness accounts give testimony to the great spiritual joy that seemed to overflow from St Philip's heart, and was evident to everyone who met him.

Often times this joy would have physical manifestations: some witnesses report seeing St Philip levitate at the altar while saying Mass, and the servers who assisted at his Mass later in his life tell us that, when he came to the elevation of the Host before Communion, he would sometimes be lost in contemplation for hours at a time. People who came to his room early in the morning for confession often found him lost in prayer, perhaps standing in the middle of the room with his shirt half-buttoned, so distracted by love and joy that he had forgotten what he was doing.

We have seen already, though, that St Philip did not put much stock in these ecstatic gifts and manifestations in his own life, and he positively discouraged them in others. "He who desires ecstasies and visions does not know what he is desiring," he would say, and he meant it. The raptures that used to come upon him while he was preaching or celebrating Mass were a source of great embarrassment and distress for him, and he would do anything he could think of to distract himself so that his emotions did not overpower him. With others he was equally cautious.

"Philip did not make much account of this warmth and acuteness of feeling, for he said that emotion was not devotion, that tears were no sign that a man was in the grace of God; neither must we suppose a man holy merely because he weeps when he speaks of religion."

Still, the holy joy that filled St Philip's heart was difficult to hide, and in many cases was positively contagious. "What St Paul says of himself seemed to be fulfilled in Philip," Newman tells us, quoting the second letter to the Corinthians: "I am filled with consolation - I over-abound with joy." His penitents often felt joyful simply being in his room, even if he were not there, and some who were in distress only needed to stand at the door of his room, without going in, to feel better. Though some people are naturally outgoing and expressive, it seems that this was not the case with St Philip, and he was always ready to attribute the joy he felt and shared with others to its real source. "The Holy Spirit is the master of prayer and causes us to abide in continual peace and cheerfulness, which is a foretaste of Paradise. We ought to pray God fervently to increase in us every day the light and heat of his goodness."

Litany

Our Father, Hail Mary, Glory be.

Concluding Prayer

Heavenly Father, hear the prayers that we make
    in the name of your Son,
and give us the Paraclete whom he promised
    you would send.
May we rejoice always in the presence of your Holy Spirit,
and become living signs of his action in the world.
We ask this through Christ our Lord. Amen.

Day Three - Peace

Hymn (*See pp.187-190*)

Antiphon

Come, Holy Spirit, fill the hearts of your faithful, and kindle in them the fire of your love.
Send forth your Spirit,
and they will be created,
- And you will renew the face of the earth.

Prayer

Father of mercy, your Holy Spirit is the sign and instrument of your peace in the world.
Fill our hearts with this peace,
so that, like St Philip,
we may conform our lives to your holy will.
We ask this through Christ our Lord.
Amen.

Reading   (*Philippians 4:5b-7,9*)

The Lord is near. Have no anxiety at all, but in everything, by prayer and petition, with thanksgiving, make your requests known to God. Then the peace of God that surpasses all understanding will guard your hearts and minds in Christ Jesus. ...Keep on doing what you have learned and received and heard and seen in me. Then the God of peace will be with you.

Responsory

(cf. Romans 5:5; 8:11)

The love of God has been poured into our hearts (alleluia).

- By his Spirit living in us (alleluia).

Meditation

"He who wishes for anything but Christ does not know what he wishes; he who asks for anything but Christ does not know what he is asking; he who works, and not for Christ, does not know what he is doing." Such single-mindedness lies at the heart of St Philip's approach to life and ministry, and gives us insight into the source of the peace which pervaded his personality. St Thomas says that the peace that is a fruit of the Holy Spirit involves two things: "freedom from outward disturbance", since our hearts are so fixed on God that they do not attend to external things; and perfect calm, since "our desires rest altogether in one object," namely, doing God's will. St Philip was aware that God required not only all of his love, but also his full attention and complete confidence; because he was able to give them, he enjoyed real peace. "To be entirely conformed and resigned to the divine will is truly a road in which we cannot go wrong, and is the only road which leads us to taste and enjoy that peace which sensual and earthly men know nothing of."

But how does one know that he is truly resigned to the divine will? For St Philip the answer lay in distrusting the self, and putting complete confidence in one's spiritual director. He insisted that the primary relationship in the life of anyone striving for virtue is one of obedience to the spiritual father. "He always asked advice, even on affairs of minor importance. His constant counsel to his penitents was, that they should not trust in themselves, but always take the advice of others, and get as many prayers as they could." "They who really wish to advance in the way of God," he said, "must give themselves up into the hands of their superiors always and in everything. …There is nothing which gives greater security to our actions, or more effectively cuts the snares the devil lays for us, than to follow another person's will, rather than our own, in doing good."

One anecdote shows how seriously St Philip took his own counsel in regard to obedience. He was on friendly terms with Ignatius of Loyola, who came to visit him often with letters from a fellow Jesuit, Francis Xavier, who was working as a missionary in India and the Far East. As he listened to St Ignatius read these letters, St Philip found himself burning with desire to follow in St Francis's footsteps, and there came a time when he had gathered twenty or so men and was ready to set sail with them for pagan territories. But he would not go until he had consulted a priest whom he had come to trust. This priest told St Philip, "Your Indies are in Rome," and he accepted the advice with peaceful resignation. This conversation took place in 1556; for the next forty years, St Philip worked diligently in Rome and never left the city.

As a spiritual director himself, St Philip often shared this gift of peace with those who turned to him for guidance. Some "recovered their lost peace of mind by simply looking Philip in the face. To dream of him was enough to comfort many. In a word, Philip was a perpetual refreshment to all those who were in perplexity and sadness." Because of this he was in great demand as a counsellor and confessor, and his penitents gave him little rest, even when he was sick. But he held nothing back from those who needed to know God's peace; indeed, Newman tells us, "when he was ill, he did not so much receive as impart consolation."

Litany

Our Father, Hail Mary, Glory be.

Concluding Prayer

Heavenly Father, hear the prayers that we make in the name of your Son,
and give us the Paraclete
    whom he promised you would send.
    May the peace that your Holy Spirit brings
    transform our lives, remove anxiety,
    and teach us to be obedient to you.
    We ask this through Christ our Lord.
    Amen.

Hymn (*See pp.187-190*)

Antiphon

Come, Holy Spirit, fill the hearts of your faithful, and kindle in them the fire of your love.
Send forth your Spirit,
and they will be created,
- And you will renew the face of the earth.

Prayer

Father, the grace of your Holy Spirit gives us courage to endure all things. Strengthen our hearts, that like St Philip, we may patiently endure every trial, and persevere in doing your will. We ask this through Christ our Lord. Amen.

Reading   (*James 5:7-8*)

Be patient, therefore, brothers, until the coming of the Lord. See how the farmer waits for the precious fruit of the earth, being patient with it until it receives the early and the late rains. You too must be patient. Make your hearts firm, because the coming of the Lord is at hand.

Responsory   (*cf. Romans 5:5; 8:11*)

The love of God has been poured into our hearts (alleluia).

- By his Spirit living in us (alleluia).

Meditation

The way that St Philip dealt with his own illnesses, which were many, points us to another fruit that the Spirit bore in his life: namely, patience. The Vulgate translation of the Scriptures adds another fruit here, called long-suffering, and St Thomas distinguishes the two in this way: each, he says, refer to the ability of the mind not to be disturbed. Patience, properly so-called, endures when evil threatens; long-suffering perseveres when good things are delayed. Both aspects of patience were central to St Philip's spirituality. "The great matter," he insisted over and over, "is to persevere."

Certainly patience is necessary in the midst of physical suffering - "Resignation is all in all to the sick man" - but it applies equally to spiritual tribulations, persecutions and misunderstandings as well. St Philip was no stranger to this kind of suffering: on more than one occasion those who misunderstood his efforts or were jealous of his success (often the same people) went out of their way to make life difficult for him, even going so far as to report him to the Holy See as a suspected heretic. Each time he was vindicated and given reassurance, often by the Holy Father himself, but the hurt was real. Still, he saw everything he suffered as part of God's plan, and welcomed it with love.

"There is no surer or clearer proof of the love of God than adversity," he advised. "Tribulations, if we bear them patiently for the love of God, appear bitter at first, but they grow sweet when one gets accustomed to the taste."

He likewise advised his penitents to make patience and long-suffering a part of their prayer life:

"We must not give up praying because we do not receive what we ask for all at once." Not only did they need to have patience when asking something from God and waiting for it to be fulfilled, but they ought, he said, to make perseverance itself the object of their request. "Among the things we ought to ask of God is perseverance in well-doing and in serving the Lord, because, if we only have patience and persevere in the good life we have begun to lead, we shall acquire a most eminent degree of spirituality. We must often remember what Christ said, that not he who begins, but he who perseveres to the end, shall be saved."

Litany

Our Father, Hail Mary, Glory be.

Concluding Prayer

Heavenly Father, hear the prayers that we make in the name of your Son,
and give us the Paraclete whom he promised   you would send.
May that Holy Spirit be our strength when we are weak,
and help us to bear patiently whatever you ask of us.
We ask this through Christ our Lord.
Amen.

Day Five - Kindness

Hymn *(See pp.187-190)*

Antiphon

Come, Holy Spirit, fill the hearts of your faithful, and kindle in them the fire of your love.
Send forth your Spirit,
and they will be created,
- And you will renew the face of the earth.

Prayer

Merciful Father, your kindness endures forever. May the same Holy Spirit who filled the heart
of St Philip fill our hearts also,
and make himself known in the kindness
we show to those around us.
We ask this through Christ our Lord. Amen.

Reading

(Ephesians 4:30-32)

Do not grieve the Spirit of God, with which you have been sealed for the day of redemption. All bitterness, fury, anger, shouting, and reviling must be removed from you, along with all malice. And be kind to one another, compassionate, forgiving one another as God has forgiven you in Christ.

Responsory

(cf. Romans 5:5; 8:11)

The love of God has been poured into our hearts (alleluia).

- By his Spirit living in us (alleluia).

Meditation

The words that St Thomas uses to discuss the fruit of kindness - also called benignity - are particularly apt in this discussion of the saint with the "heart of fire". Kindness disposes a person to treat other people well, "for the benign are those in whom the salutary flame (*bonus ignis*) of love has enkindled the desire to be kind to their neighbour." The flame of love in St Philip showed itself constantly in the cheerful kindness which he showed to all those around him, so much so that Newman can call him "winning saint" and "sweetest of fathers" without exaggeration.

A poem that the cardinal wrote about his patron has become a favourite hymn of the Oratory, and begins, "This is the saint of gentleness and kindness". "Cheerfulness strengthens the heart," St Philip says, and so "in dealing with our neighbour we must assume as much pleasantness of manner as we can, and by this affability win him to the ways of virtue."

He was convinced that the way to win someone over was by kindness, rather than harshness, and so far this approach seems obvious. He advised priests hearing confessions to be compassionate, and dozens of his penitents bear witness that he followed his own advice. But St Philip's kindness was not affected or insincere; rather, we find its source in his real humility, and in his basic conviction that he was addressing Christ in every person whom he encountered. He was kind to friends and strangers alike: "Philip welcomed those who consulted him with singular benignity, and received them, though strangers, with as much affection as if he had been a long time expecting them."

In dealing with others, benignity requires that we always assume the best of them, and not impute bad motives to the things we see them do. "We should never remind anyone of his natural defects," St Philip counsels, and "we must sometimes bear with little defects in others. We should not be quick at correcting others; we ought to hate no one." Several centuries later, Cardinal Newman would incorporate these and similar sentiments into his definition of a gentleman (*The Idea of a University*). Kindness is at the heart of the community life that is the essence of the Congregation of the Oratory, and a necessary protection against the dangers that threaten fraternal love. "Our enemy, the devil, who fights with us in order to vanquish us, seeks to disunite us in our houses and to breed quarrels, dislikes, contests, and rivalries… While we are fighting with each other, he comes and conquers us and makes us more securely his own."

But cheerful kindness was not something St Philip advised merely for the sake of winning others. It likewise strengthens the heart of the one who practises it, for by being cheerful we are co-operating with the Spirit of kindness, and allowing the "salutary flame of love" to bear fruit in our actions. "The true way to advance in holy virtues is to persevere in a holy cheerfulness," he says, and "the cheerful are much easier to guide in the spiritual life than the melancholy." The connection between cheerful kindness and growth in spirituality is found in the freedom that comes with humility, and St Philip saw a lack of cheerfulness to be connected with too much self-concern. "Excessive sadness," he insisted, "seldom springs from any other source than pride."

Litany

Our Father, Hail Mary, Glory be.

Concluding Prayer

Heavenly Father, hear the prayers that we make in the name of your Son, and give us the Paraclete whom he promised you would send. Set our hearts on fire with your Holy Spirit, and help us to share this flame of love with our brothers and sisters. We ask this through Christ our Lord. Amen.

Day Six - Goodness

Hymn (*See pp.187-190*)

Antiphon

Come, Holy Spirit, fill the hearts of your faithful, and kindle in them the fire of your love.
Send forth your Spirit, and they will be created,
- And you will renew the face of the earth.

Prayer

Loving Father, your generous love overflows in the outpouring of your Holy Spirit.
Fill us, as you filled St Philip,
with the Spirit of generosity,
and teach us to make a gift of ourselves to others.
We ask this through Christ our Lord. Amen.

Reading
(1 Timothy 6:18-19)

Tell the rich in the present age not to be proud and not to rely on so uncertain a thing as wealth, but rather on God, who richly provides us with all things for our enjoyment. Tell them to do good, to be rich in good works, to be generous, ready to share, thus accumulating as treasure a good foundation for the future, so as to win the life that is true life.

Responsory
(cf. Romans 5:5; 8:11)

The love of God has been poured into our hearts (alleluia).
- By his Spirit living in us (alleluia).

Meditation

Like kindness and cheerfulness, the spiritual fruit of goodness also disposes us well towards our neighbour; here, the Spirit is at work to produce not only good thoughts towards others, but a willingness to do good things for those around us. "Do not let a day pass without doing some good during it," St Philip advised his disciples. "We must not delay in doing good, for death will not delay its time." He felt an urgency about making the love of God and neighbour visible in the form of good works, and this was a watchword with him from the very beginning of his time in Rome. When he met young men on his walks during those early days in Rome, his greeting was always the same: "Well!" he would say, with a grin on his face, "When shall we have a mind to begin to do good?"

This goodness requires a generous spirit, one that is sincerely detached from the world and its material delights. "Give me ten men who are really detached from the world, and wish for nothing but Christ," St Philip once exclaimed, "and I have the heart to believe I could convert the world with them." But the freedom and power that come with detachment are completely squelched by the bonds of avarice.

"He who wishes for material possessions will never have devotion. ...He who wishes for perfection must have no attachments to anything of this world."

Anecdotes abound of the counsels he gave and the penances he assigned, to gently but firmly lead those who were greedy to renounce their connections to material things. Generosity for St Philip applied not merely to money and objects - he had few enough of them as it was, and often showed his gratitude for gifts by giving one to the donor that was double the value of the one he had received. More important for him was a commitment to be generous with his time and energy. "If we wish to help our neighbour," he taught, "we must reserve for ourselves neither place, nor hour, nor time." When one of the fathers of the Congregation refused to answer the door to those who came for confession or alms, because he was saying his prayers, St Philip would have none of it.

He admonished him and the other fathers and brothers that when they were called for, they were to come immediately, no matter if they were praying or anything else, for in doing so they would be "leaving Christ for Christ."

Litany

Our Father, Hail Mary, Glory be.

Concluding Prayer

Heavenly Father, hear the prayers that we make
in the name of your Son,
and give us the Paraclete
whom he promised you would send.
Let the love of your Holy Spirit abound in our hearts,
and help us to bear fruit in good works
and generous service to our neighbour.
We ask this through Christ our Lord.
Amen.

Day Seven - Faithfulness

Hymn (*See pp.187-190*)

Antiphon

Come, Holy Spirit, fill the hearts of your faithful, and kindle in them the fire of your love.
Send forth your Spirit,
and they will be created,
- And you will renew the face of the earth.

Prayer

Holy Father, your love for us is everlasting and always true.
By the gift of your Holy Spirit
keep us faithful to you,
that in imitation of St Philip
we may serve you with integrity.
We ask this through Christ our Lord.
Amen.

Reading
(Revelation 2:10b, 25-26)

Remain faithful until death, and I will give you the crown of life… You must hold fast to what you have until I come. To the victor, who keeps my ways until the end, I will give authority over the nations.

Responsory
(cf. Romans 5:5; 8:11)

The love of God has been poured into our hearts (alleluia).
- By his Spirit living in us, (alleluia).

Meditation

St Thomas tells us that the spiritual fruit of fidelity, or faithfulness, has two aspects. On the one hand, fidelity toward our neighbour keeps us from offending him through fraud or deceit. Faithfulness toward God is closely connected with the supernatural virtue of faith, and leads us to subject our intellect, and all that we have, to God. St Philip bore the spiritual fruit of faithfulness equally toward God and his neighbour, providing an example and instruction for his disciples to do the same.

We have seen how gentle and kind St Philip always was toward those around him. He also demanded absolute honesty and integrity in his relationships. "He could not bear two-faced persons," Cardinal Newman tells us, and "as for liars, he could not endure them, and was continually reminding his spiritual children to avoid them as they would a pestilence." Lying to avoid embarrassment was even worse; he insisted that his followers accept the crosses that came to them daily, since "he who runs away from the Cross the Lord sends him" through daily humiliations "will meet a bigger one on the road." The faithfulness that St Philip practised and demanded of others was not relaxed in the face of adversity or hardship. On the contrary, he insisted, "poverty and tribulations are given us by God as trials of our fidelity."

St Philip recognised how difficult it is to maintain this fidelity, especially toward God, in the face of trials. "Everyone is willing to stand on Mount Tabor and see Christ transfigured, but few are willing to go up to Jerusalem and accompany Christ to Mount Calvary." Therefore he counselled his followers that the best way to be faithful was to start slowly and focus on perseverance, rather than try to take on too much at the beginning, and burn out quickly. "We must not be too ready to trust young men who have great devotion," he said, speaking from experience. "We must wait till their wings are grown and then see what sort of a flight they make." When someone came to him full of fire and enthusiasm, he did not crush their good intentions, but he urged them to proceed with moderation. "It is well to choose some one good devotion and stick to it," he advised. "We must not wish to do everything at once, or become a saint in four days, but gradually, little by little."

Litany

Our Father, Hail Mary, Glory be.

Concluding Prayer

Heavenly Father, hear the prayers that we make
in the name of your Son,
and give us the Paraclete
whom he promised you would send.
Keep us faithful to you,
that filled with your grace we may serve
and worship you in Spirit and in truth.
We ask this through Christ our Lord.
Amen.

Day Eight - Gentleness

Hymn (*See pp.187-190*)

Antiphon

Come, Holy Spirit, fill the hearts of your faithful, and
kindle in them the fire of your love.
Send forth your Spirit,
and they will be created,
- And you will renew the face of the earth.

Prayer

Gentle Father, your justice is revealed in mercy,
and your power in forgiveness.
May the same Holy Spirit
who filled the gentle heart of St Philip,
teach us to reach out to others with his tender love.
We ask this through Christ our Lord.
Amen.

Reading   *(Ephesians 4:1-4a)*

I then, a prisoner for the Lord, urge you to live in a
manner worthy of the call you have received, with
all humility and gentleness, bearing with one another
through love, striving to preserve the unity of the spirit
through the bond of peace: one body and one Spirit.

Responsory   *(cf. Romans 5:5; 8:11)*

The love of God has been poured into our hearts
(alleluia).

- By his Spirit living in us (alleluia).

Meditation

Gentleness allows a person to suffer "with equanimity the evils which his neighbour inflicts on him," says St Thomas, and to curb anger. This meekness and gentle spirit was evident in St Philip throughout his life, even when he had become the first Provost or father of the newly-formed Congregation of the Oratory. He did not allow himself to get puffed up with pride because of the authority which he exercised - his advice was that "he who wishes to be perfectly obeyed should give but few orders" - and advised his followers that in all things "a man should keep himself down, and not busy himself *in mirabilibus super se* [in marvels beyond his power]."

St Philip's gentleness allowed him to remain calm even when those around him - sometimes even those closest to him - did not treat him with the respect that he deserved. A famous story is related about Father Talpa, one of the first Oratorians. As Newman tells it, "Once, when he was Superior of the Congregation, one of his subjects snatched a letter out of his hand; but the saint took the affront with incomparable meekness, and neither in look, nor word, nor in gesture betrayed the slightest emotion."

Although this may have amazed his other disciples, St Philip demanded that they always follow his example when it came to this kind of mortification. "He who wishes to become a saint must never defend himself. ... He who cannot put up with the loss of his honour can never advance." In order to instill this attitude in his disciples, St Philip insisted on the mortification of the *razionale*, the reasoning part of the mind that always wants to have its way, to be given explanations and consulted on matters. To mortify this part of the self was, for St Philip, much more important than external mortifications like fasting, vigils and bodily penances.

Whenever someone asked him why his disciples did not fast, "he was accustomed to say, 'The sanctity of a man lies within the space of three fingers,' and, while he said it, he would touch his forehead, and add, in explanation of his words, 'The whole point lies in mortifying the understanding ... since perfection consists in leading captive our own will and following that of our superiors" (from *The Excellences of the Oratory*).

The penances that St Philip assigned to some of those who came to him for confession are legendary: for example, those who struggled with vanity often found themselves ordered to dress in their best attire and carry St Philip's dog in their arms through the city streets, with a procession of street urchins mocking them all the way. In this manner he hoped to teach his penitents not to be worried about the opinion others had of them, and to "keep down and thwart [that] touchiness of mind" that is a sure sign of pride, and that leads to unkind and ungentle behaviour. Above all else, the struggle to bear the spiritual fruit of meekness and gentleness requires a sense of humour, especially regarding ourselves and our own status. "To persevere in our cheerfulness amid ...troubles is a sign of a right and good spirit."

Litany

Our Father, Hail Mary, Glory be.

Concluding Prayer

Heavenly Father, hear the prayers that we make
in the name of your Son,
and give us the Paraclete
    whom he promised you would send.
May your Holy Spirit teach us to conquer our pride,
and to spend our lives in humble,
gentle service to our brothers and sisters.
We ask this through Christ our Lord.
Amen.

Day Nine - Self-Control

Hymn (*See pp.187-190*)

Antiphon

Come, Holy Spirit, fill the hearts of your faithful, and kindle in them the fire of your love.
Send forth your Spirit,
and they will be created,
- And you will renew the face of the earth.

Prayer

Father, the wisdom and strength of your Holy Spirit made St Philip a model of chastity
to inspire those around him.
May that same Spirit strengthen us in mind and body,
and teach us to serve you with pure hearts.
We ask this through Christ our Lord. Amen.

Reading   (*Galatians 5:16-17, 24-25*)

I say, then: live by the Spirit and you will certainly not gratify the desire of the flesh. For the flesh has desires against the Spirit, and the Spirit against the flesh …Now those who belong to Christ have crucified their flesh with its passions and desires. If we live in the Spirit, let us also follow the Spirit.

Responsory   (*cf. Romans 5:5; 8:11*)

The love of God has been poured into our hearts (alleluia).

- By his Spirit living in us (alleluia).

Meditation

The spiritual fruit of continence, or self-control, is closely connected with the virtue of temperance, and means that the Holy Spirit working in us gives us power to control our bodily desires, and to keep both soul and body in their proper relationship. The Vulgate translation of the letter to the Galatians adds two more spiritual fruits here - modesty and chastity which further specify the self-control which continence involves, and draw our attention to the importance of integrity and vigilance with regard to sexuality. In St Philip's time, as in our own, chastity was not a "fashionable" virtue, as the art and philosophy of the late Renaissance humanists seemed to revive all of the excesses of ancient paganism. The continence that St Philip displayed in his own life, and encouraged in the lives of others, gives evidence of the power of the Holy Spirit at work in him.

Those who gave testimony during the process of St Philip's canonisation noted over and over the great purity which was evident in his whole demeanour - so much so that, as Cardinal Newman tells us, "it shone out of his countenance. His eyes were so clear and bright, even to the last years of his life, that no painter ever succeeded in giving the expression of them… Moreover, his body, even in his old age, emitted a fragrance which refreshed those who came near him." All of his biographers relate that St Philip maintained his virginity throughout his life, despite many attempts by those who were jealous of him to trip him up. His constant approach was to avoid the source of the temptation; he always said that "in the warfare of the flesh, only cowards gain the victory; that is, those who flee."

This was his advice to his penitents as well, for he believed that "in the matter of purity, there is no greater danger than not fearing the danger." "When a person puts himself in the occasion of sin, saying, 'I shall not fall, I shall not commit it,' it is an almost infallible sign that he will fall, and with all the greater damage to his soul." And so he gave his followers some very practical rules for daily living, which were no doubt drawn from years of his own experience: they needed good friends, but should avoid bad company; they were not to retire to their rooms immediately after the mid-day meal; they must avoid idleness. When faced with a sudden temptation, they should fix their minds on something else, no matter what, and use little prayers like "God, come to my assistance. Lord, make haste to help me." Above all, he insisted, frequent use of the Sacrament of Reconciliation was central to the battle for chastity.

"A most excellent means of keeping ourselves pure is to lay open all our thoughts, as soon as possible, to our confessor, with the greatest sincerity, and keep nothing hidden in ourselves. To acquire and preserve the virtue of chastity, we have need of a good and experienced confessor."

This was St Philip's special ministry, and in the confessional he used every gift and fruit of the Spirit to bring souls back to God. It is said that he had a supernatural ability to know who had committed sins against chastity by their smell, and at times he would tell a penitent who was embarrassed and hesitant to confess, "My son, I know your sins already."

Notwithstanding his own strict virtue, and this ability to detect the stench of sin, he treated those who came to him to confess sins of impurity with the utmost compassion. "One of the most efficacious means of keeping chaste," he said, "is to have compassion for those who fall through their frailty, and never to boast in the least of being free." He insisted that his disciples treat each other with the same patient understanding, and he used to say that "not to have pity for another in such cases was a forerunner of a speedy fall in ourselves; and that when he found a man censorious, and secure of himself, and without fear, he gave him up for lost."

By his tender guidance St Philip helped many young men to make a good confession and to be set free from years' worth of bad habits and serious sins, and their connection with him enabled them to persevere in chastity. "Many confessed that they were at once delivered from temptations by his merely laying his hands on their heads. The very mention of his name had a power of shielding from Satan those who were assailed by his fiery darts."

Litany

Our Father, Hail Mary, Glory be.

Concluding Prayer

Heavenly Father, hear the prayers that we make in the name of your Son,
and give us the Paraclete
   whom he promised you would send.
May your Holy Spirit cleanse our hearts
   and strengthen our bodies.
May the purity of our lives bear witness
   to the power of your love.
We ask this through Christ our Lord.
Amen.

Hymns

Come, Holy Ghost

Come Holy Ghost, Creator Blest,
And in our hearts take up Thy rest;
Come with Thy grace and heav'nly aid
To fill the hearts which Thou hast made,
To fill the hearts which Thou hast made.
O Comforter, to Thee we cry,
Thou heav'nly Gift of God most high;
Thou fount of life and fire of love,
And sweet anointing from above,
And sweet anointing from above.
O Holy Ghost, Through thee alone
Know we the Father and the Son;
Be this our firm unchanging creed:
That thou dost from them both proceed,
That thou dost from them both proceed.
Praise be to Thee Father and Son,
And Holy Spirit Three in one;
And may the Son on us bestow
The gifts that from the Spirit flow,
The gifts that from the Spirit flow.

(Text from the Veni Creator Spiritus.
Translated by Fr Edward Caswall of the Oratory)

Veni Creator Spiritus

Come, Holy Spirit, Creator come,
From your bright heavenly throne!
Come, take possession of our souls,
And make them all your own.

You who are called the Paraclete,
Best gift of God above,
The living spring, the living fire,
Sweet unction, and true love!

You who are sevenfold in your grace,
Finger of God's right hand,
His promise, teaching little ones
To speak and understand!

O guide our minds with your blessed light,
With love our hearts inflame,
And with your strength which never decays
Confirm our mortal frame.

Far from us drive our hellish foe
True peace unto us bring,
And through all perils guide us safe
Beneath your sacred wing.

Through you may we the Father know,
Through you the eternal Son
And you the Spirit of them both
Thrice-blessed three in one.

All glory to the Father be,
And to the risen Son;
The same to you, O Paraclete,
While endless ages run. Amen.

Veni, creátor Spíritus,
mentes tuórum vísita,
imple supérna grátia,
quæ tu creásti péctora.

Qui díceris Paráclitus,
altíssimi donum Dei,
fons vivus, ignis, cáritas,
et spiritális únctio.

Tu septifórmis múnere,
dígitus patérnæ déxteræ,
tu rite promíssum Patris,
sermóne ditans gúttura.

Accénde lumen sénsibus,
infúnde amórem córdibus,
infírma nostri córporis
virtúte firmans pérpeti.

Hostem repéllas lóngius
pacémque dones prótinus;
ductóre sic te prævio
vitémus omne nóxium.

Per Te sciámus da Patrem
noscámus atque Fílium,
teque utriúsque Spíritum
credámus omni témpore.

Deo Patri sit glória,
et Fílio, qui a mórtuis
surréxit, ac Paráclito,
in sæculórum sæcula. Amen.

(Attributed to Rabanus Maurus - 766-856)

Hymn to St Philip

This is the saint of gentleness and kindness,
Cheerful in penance, and in precept winning;
Patiently healing of their pride and blindness
Souls that are sinning.
This is the saint who, when the world allures us,
Cries her false wares, and opes her magic coffers,
Points to a better city, and secures us
With richer offers.
Love is his bond; he knows no other fetter,
Asks not our all, but takes whate'er we spare him,
Willing to draw us on from good to better,
As we can bear him.
When he comes near to teach us and to bless us,
Prayer is so sweet that hours are but a minute;
Mirth is so pure, though freely it possess us,
Sin is not in it.
Thus he conducts by holy paths and pleasant
Innocent souls, and sinful souls forgiven,
Towards the bright palace where our God is present,
Throned in high heaven.
This is the saint of gentleness and kindness,
Cheerful in penance, and in precept winning;
Patiently healing of their pride and blindness
Souls that are sinning.

(John Henry Newman)

Litany of the Holy Spirit

Lord, have mercy. *Lord, have mercy.*
Christ, have mercy. *Christ, have mercy.*
Lord, have mercy. *Lord, have mercy.*
Christ, hear us. *Christ, graciously hear us.*
God the Father of Heaven, *Have mercy on us. (repeat)*
God the Son, Redeemer of the world,
God the Holy Spirit,
Holy Trinity, One God,
Holy Spirit, proceeding from the Father and the Son,
Holy Spirit, co-equal with the Father and the Son,
Promise of the Father, most bounteous,
Ray of Heavenly Light,
Author of all good,
Source of living Water,
Consuming Fire,
Burning Love,
Spiritual Unction,
Spirit of truth and power,
Spirit of wisdom and understanding,
Spirit of counsel and fortitude,
Spirit of knowledge and piety,
Spirit of fear of the Lord,
Spirit of compunction,
Spirit of grace and prayer,
Spirit of love, peace and joy,
Spirit of patience,
Spirit of longanimity and goodness,
Spirit of benignity and mildness,
Spirit of fidelity,
Spirit of modesty and continence,
Spirit of chastity,
Spirit of adoption of sons of God,
Holy Spirit, our Comforter,

Holy Spirit, our Sanctifier, *Have mercy on us. (repeat)*
You who in the beginning moved upon the waters,
You through whom spoke holy men of God,
You who overshadowed the Virgin Mary,
You by whom Mary conceived Christ,
You who descend upon men at Baptism,
You who, on the Day of Pentecost appeared through
    fiery tongues,
You by whom we are reborn,
You who dwell in us as in a Temple,
You who govern and animate the Church,
You who fill the whole world,
That you will renew the face of the earth,
We beseech you, hear us. (repeat)
That you may shed your Light upon us,
That you may pour your Love into our hearts,
That you may inspire us to love our neighbour,
That you may teach us to ask for the graces we need,
That you may enlighten us

    with your heavenly inspirations,
That you may guide us in the way of holiness,
That you may make us obedient
    to your commandments,
That you may teach us how to pray,
That you may always pray with us,
That you may inspire us with horror for sin,
That you may direct us in the practice of virtue,
That you may make us persevere in a holy life,
That you may make us faithful to our vocation,
That you may grant us good priests and bishops,
That you may give us good Christian families,
That you may grant us a spiritual renewal
    of the Church,
That you may guide and console the Holy Father,

Lamb of God, who takes away the sins of the world:
Spare us, O Lord.
Lamb of God, who takes away the sins of the world:
Graciously hear us, O Lord.
Lamb of God, who takes away the sins of the world:
Have mercy on us.
Holy Spirit, hear us.
Holy Spirit, Graciously hear us.
Lord, have mercy. *Lord, have mercy.*
Christ, have mercy. *Christ, have mercy.*
Lord, have mercy. *Lord, have mercy.*
Create a clean heart in us, O Lord.
Renew a right spirit in us, O Lord.

Let us pray:

O God, who enlightens the hearts of the faithful
by the light of the Holy Spirit,
grant to us the same Spirit,
that we may be truly wise and ever rejoice
in his consolation.
We ask this through Christ our Lord.
Amen.

The Litany of St Philip

Lord, have mercy. *Lord, have mercy.*
Christ, have mercy. *Christ, have mercy.*
Lord, have mercy. *Lord, have mercy.*
Christ, hear us. *Christ, graciously hear us.*
God the Father of heaven, *Have mercy on us.*
God the Son, Redeemer of the World,
Have mercy on us.
God the Holy Ghost, *Have mercy on us.*
Holy Trinity, One God, *Have mercy on us.*
Holy Mary, *Pray for us. (repeat)*
Holy Mother of God,
Holy Virgin of Virgins,
St Philip,
Vessel of the Holy Ghost,
Child of Mary,
Apostle of Rome,
Counsellor of Popes,
Voice of prophecy,
Man of primitive times,
Winning saint,
Hidden hero,
Sweetest of fathers,
Flower of purity,
Martyr of charity,
Heart of fire,
Discerner of spirits,
Choicest of priests,
Mirror of the divine life,
Pattern of humility,
Example of simplicity,
Light of holy joy,
Image of childhood,
Picture of old age,
Director of souls,

Gentle guide of youth, *Pray for us. (repeat)*
Patron of thine own,
Who didst observe chastity in thy youth,
Who didst seek Rome by divine guidance,
Who didst hide so long in the Catacombs,
Who didst receive the Holy Ghost into thy heart,
Who didst experience such wonderful ecstasies,
Who didst so lovingly serve the little ones,
Who didst wash the feet of pilgrims,
Who didst ardently thirst after martyrdom,
Who didst distribute the daily word of God,
Who didst turn so many hearts to God,
Who didst converse so sweetly with Mary,
Who didst raise the dead,
Who didst set up thy houses in all lands,
Lamb of God, who takest away the sins of the world,
Spare us, O Lord.
Lamb of God, who takest away the sins of the world,
Graciously hear us, O Lord.
Lamb of God, who takest away the sins of the world,
Have mercy on us.
Christ, hear us.
Christ, graciously hear us.

> V. Remember thy Congregation,
>
> R. Which thou hast possessed from the beginning.

Let us pray:

O God, who hast exalted blessed Philip,
thy Confessor, in the glory of thy saints,
grant that, as we rejoice in his commemoration, so we
may profit by the example of his virtues,
through Christ our Lord.
R. Amen.

LITANIES
TO THE SAINTS

Litanies - A Short History

How litanies developed

A litany is simply a prayer. The word derives from the Greek *lite* which means "supplication". This gave rise to the word *litaneia*, "prayer, entreaty"; and this word, in turn, made its way via its late Latin form, *litania*, into our own language. Specifically, it now refers to a certain form of prayer as repetitive dialogue, which has its roots both in the natural inclination of humanity to find many and various ways of praising and making supplication to its deities, and also more particularly in the human response of gratitude to the supernatural revelation God gives of himself to his people.

Litany of the Saints

Pope Gregory the Great seems to have formalised this litany which was already popular, declaring that it be sung for three days at the start of Lent as well as other times. The Litany of the Saints was also used in a thanksgiving procession he ordered for the end of a great plague in 590.

This litany is used in our own liturgy. We find it incorporated (in an abridged form) into the Easter Vigil on Holy Saturday, into Ordination Masses, and used on Rogation Days (now optional, so not often observed) and around the time of All Saints and All Souls. It is used also for special occasions, such as the consecration of a church and at the funeral of a Pope. Many people will remember the moving and beautiful singing of this litany at the transferral of the body of St John Paul II to the Basilica of St Peter in 2005.

The saints included in this litany predate the canonisation process we know today; saints were declared as such by popular acclamation and by martyrdom. The number of saints included has grown over the years, and often saints are added for particular occasions and needs.

The Litany

In the name of the Father and of the Son and of the Holy Spirit.
Amen.

Lord, have mercy. *Lord, have mercy.*
Christ, have mercy. *Christ, have mercy.*
Lord, have mercy. *Lord, have mercy.*
Holy Mary, Mother of God, *Pray for us. (repeat)*
Holy Virgin of virgins,
St Michael,
Holy angels of God,
Abraham, our father in faith,
David, leader of God's people,
All holy patriarchs and prophets,
St John the Baptist,
St Joseph,
St Peter and St Paul,
St Andrew,
St John,
St Mary Magdalen,
St Stephen,
St Ignatius of Antioch,
St Lawrence,
St Perpetua and St Felicity,
St Agnes,
St Gregory,
St Augustine,
St Athanasius,
St Basil,
St Martin,
St Benedict,
St Francis and St Dominic,
St Francis Xavier,
St John Vianney,

St Catherine of Siena, *Pray for us. (repeat)*
St Teresa of Jesus,

Other saints maybe included here

All holy men and women, saints of God, *Pray for us*
Lord, be merciful, *Lord, deliver us we pray*
From all evil, *Lord, save your people (repeat)*
From every sin,
From Satan's power,
At the moment of death,
From everlasting death,
On the day of judgement,
By your Incarnation,
By your suffering and Cross,
By your Death and Resurrection,
By your return in glory to the Father,
By the outpouring of the Holy Spirit,
By your coming again in glory,

Be merciful to us sinners,
Lord, we ask you, hear our prayer (repeat)
Guide and protect your holy Church,
Keep the Pope and all the clergy in faithful service
to your Church,
Bring all peoples together in love and peace,
Strengthen us in your service,
Jesus, Son of the Living God,

Christ, hear us, *Christ, hear us*
Christ, graciously hear us, *Christ, graciously hear us*

Let us pray.

God of our ancestors who set their hearts on you, of those who fell asleep in peace,
and of those who won the martyrs' violent crown: we are surrounded by these witnesses
    as by clouds of fragrant incense.
In this age we would be counted
    in this communion of all the saints;
keep us always in their good and blessed company.
In their midst we make every prayer
    through Christ who is our Lord for ever and ever.
Amen.

Litany of the Sacred Heart of Jesus

This litany was authorised in 1899, by Leo XIII and is often used on the First Fridays of the month as a way of expressing sorrow for sins committed against the Sacred Heart of Jesus which is so full of love for us. St Margaret Mary had made the devotion to the Sacred Heart well known through the visions she received in 1673-1675 and several litanies developed during the following years. The litany as we now have it is an amalgamation of these, consisting of thirty-three petitions - one for each year of our Lord's life.

The Litany

In the name of the Father and of the Son and of the Holy Spirit.
Amen.

Lord, have mercy, *Lord, have mercy.*
Christ, have mercy, *Christ, have mercy.*
Lord, have mercy, *Lord, have mercy.*

God our Father of Heaven, *have mercy on us. (repeat)*
God the Son, Redeemer of the world,
God, the Holy Spirit,
Holy Trinity, One God,
Heart of Jesus, Son of the Eternal Father,
Heart of Jesus, formed by the Holy Spirit
    in the womb of the Virgin Mother,
Heart of Jesus, one with the eternal Word,
Heart of Jesus, infinite in majesty,
Heart of Jesus, holy temple of God,
Heart of Jesus, tabernacle of the Most High,
Heart of Jesus, house of God and gate of Heaven,
Heart of Jesus, aflame with love for us,

Heart of Jesus, source of justice and love,
have mercy on us. (repeat)
Heart of Jesus, full of goodness and love,
Heart of Jesus, wellspring of all virtue,
Heart of Jesus, worthy of all praise,
Heart of Jesus, king and centre of all hearts,
Heart of Jesus, treasure-house of wisdom and knowledge,
Heart of Jesus, in whom there dwells the fullness of God,
Heart of Jesus, in whom the Father is well pleased,
Heart of Jesus, pierced by a lance,
Heart of Jesus, source of all consolation,
Heart of Jesus, our life and resurrection,
Heart of Jesus, our peace and reconciliation,
Heart of Jesus, victim of our sins,
Heart of Jesus, salvation of all who trust in you,
Heart of Jesus, hope of all who die in you,
Heart of Jesus, delight of all the saints,
Heart of Jesus, from whose fullness we have all received,
Heart of Jesus, desire of the eternal hills,
Heart of Jesus, patient and full of mercy,
Heart of Jesus, generous to all who turn to you,
Heart of Jesus, fountain of life and holiness,
Heart of Jesus, atonement for our sins,
Heart of Jesus, overwhelmed with insults,
Heart of Jesus, broken for our sins,
Heart of Jesus, obedient even to death,

Lamb of God,
you take away the sins of the world, *have mercy on us.*
Lamb of God,
you take away the sins of the world, *have mercy on us.*
Lamb of God,
you take away the sins of the world, *have mercy on us.*

Jesus, meek and humble of heart.
Touch our hearts and make them like your own.

Let us pray.

Father, we rejoice in the gifts of love we have
received from the heart of Jesus your Son.
Open our hearts to share his life
and continue to bless us with his love.
We ask this in the name of Jesus the Lord. Amen.

Litany of St Joseph

This relatively recent litany was approved by Pope St Pius X on 18 March 1909. Devotion to St Joseph, whom Scripture describes as a "just man" (*Matthew* 1:19), grew throughout the twentieth century and this litany is particularly suitable for families to pray together, placing themselves under his protection. The relatively short length of this litany may also be an advantage here.

The Litany

In the name of the Father and of the Son and of the Holy Spirit.
Amen.
Lord, have mercy, *Lord, have mercy.*
Christ, have mercy, *Christ, have mercy.*
Lord, have mercy, *Lord, have mercy.*

God our Father in heaven, *have mercy on us (repeat)*
God the Son, Redeemer of the world,
God the Holy Spirit,
Holy Trinity, one God,
Holy Mary, *pray for us (repeat)*
St Joseph,
Noble son of the House of David,
Light of patriarchs,
Husband of the Mother of God,
Guardian of the Virgin,
Foster father of the Son of God,
Faithful guardian of Christ,
Head of the Holy Family,
Joseph, chaste and just,
Joseph, prudent and brave,

Joseph, obedient and loyal,
Pattern of patience,
Lover of poverty,
Model of workers,
Example to parents,
Guardian of virgins,
Pillar of family life,
Comfort of the troubled,
Hope of the sick,
Patron of the dying,
Terror of evil spirits,
Protector of the Church,

Lamb of God,
you take away the sins of the world, *have mercy on us.*
Lamb of God,
you take away the sins of the world, *have mercy on us.*
Lamb of God,
you take away the sins of the world, *have mercy on us.*

God made him master of his household,
and put him in charge of all that he owned.

Let us pray.

Almighty God, in your infinite wisdom
and love you chose Joseph
to be the husband of Mary,
the mother of your Son.
As we enjoy his protection on earth
may we have the help of his prayers in heaven.
We ask this through Christ our Lord.
Amen.

NOVENAS
TO THE SAINTS

What is a Novena?

A novena is a way of praying, often for a particular need or grace. It consists of a prayer or prayers said over nine days. The word novena is originally Latin, and means "in a group of nine". This is because a novena lasts for nine consecutive days; on each day, there is a particular prayer to be said, or devotional practice to be made.

The original novena, the model for all the rest, is the nine days between Christ's Ascension and the descent of the Holy Spirit at Pentecost, when, as we read in the Acts of the Apostles, "all these [Apostles] joined in continuous prayer, together with several women, including Mary the mother of Jesus". The Church still asks Christians to pray with particular intensity between these two feast days for the Holy Spirit to renew the Christian community.

There are many different sorts of novena; you can make a novena, perhaps to ask the intercession of a particular saint, using any prayer you want: the main thing is to pray it regularly for nine days in a row. Nevertheless most people will make a novena using a prayer composed for the purpose. Some novena prayers are long, and may include litanies, or meditations; others are short. You can make a novena using the same prayer nine times, or nine different prayers, one for each day. There are no rules; what follows are only suggestions.

The following novena prayers are addressed to individual saints, asking their intercession for whatever our intention may be. As well as interceding (praying) on our behalf, the saints are also examples of how the Christian life has been lived. Each saint experienced different events, and responded to them in different ways; we can see in their lives examples of how embracing God's will for us, whatever our individual circumstances, always brings the grace and strength from God we need to do what he asks us.

To use religious language, the saints are examples of particular virtues. In the novena prayers that follow here, we have tried for each day to take one particular virtue or quality that a saint has shown, and ask God to make it our own too, according to our needs and circumstances, and in this context to make our prayer for any particular intention we may have, whether for ourselves or for another.

Novena to St Thomas Aquinas

Feast Day: 28 January

A famous theologian, Thomas Aquinas (his surname means "from Aquino", his birthplace) was the son of an Italian nobleman. He became a member of the Dominican Order (Order of Preachers), and died in 1274 aged about fifty. Although he seemed a slow learner at first (he was fat, and habitually silent, and so was nicknamed the "dumb ox"), his teachers eventually realised he was an enormously talented theologian; he was also a man of deep prayer. He is best known for his voluminous writings, which include theological works, commentaries on Scripture, and some well-known prayers and hymns. His most famous work is the *Summa Theologiae* (Compendium of Theology), a systematic treatise covering the whole of Christian theology, which was a standard textbook until the 1960s. He was declared a Doctor of the Church in 1567. He is often considered a patron saint of study, and of education in general.

First Day: You experienced the mockery and misunderstanding of others; teach us to bear with patience, as you did, those times we receive the scorn or ridicule of others. We pray especially for [*add your intention*]. *Our Father - Hail Mary - Glory Be*

Second Day: Those who noticed only your body were surprised to learn of the great knowledge of and love for God it concealed; help us not to judge others by outward appearance, but to remember that all men and women are made in God's image and likeness. We pray especially for [*add your intention*]. *Our Father - Hail Mary - Glory Be*

Third Day: You had a great knowledge of and love for the Scriptures; help us to hear God's Word and respond to it as you did. We pray especially for [*add your intention*]. *Our Father - Hail Mary - Glory Be*

Fourth Day: You had a profound love for Christ in the Eucharist; help us, too, to experience this same reverence and love for the God who comes to us so humbly, under the forms of bread and wine. We pray especially for [*add your intention*]. *Our Father - Hail Mary - Glory Be*

Fifth Day: You did not despise the learning of the pagans, and of those of other faiths, but drew it into the service of knowing and loving the one true God, the God of Abraham, Isaac, and Jacob; help us to see God's truth wherever it is to be found, and his hand at work in all he has made. We pray especially for [*add your intention*]. *Our Father - Hail Mary - Glory Be*

Sixth Day: You gave glory to God by your writing and thought; help us to place all the works of our hands and minds at the service of God and his Church. We pray especially for [*add your intention*]. *Our Father - Hail Mary - Glory Be*

Seventh Day: You delighted to teach, and to learn; teach us to know and love God as you did, and to recognise in all we experience the signs of his overwhelming love for us. We pray especially for [*add your intention*]. *Our Father - Hail Mary - Glory Be*

Eighth Day: You were above all a man of prayer; help us to discover that it is only in a relationship of prayer that we can come to know him, who is the heart and goal of our Christian life. We pray especially for [*add your intention*]. *Our Father - Hail Mary - Glory Be*

Ninth Day: You knew that, however great our intellectual knowledge of God, it is like straw compared to the experience of his love. Help us not to let our own thoughts, concepts and plans become idols standing between us and the Father's overwhelming love for us. We pray especially for [*add your intention*]. *Our Father - Hail Mary - Glory Be*

Novena to St Josephine Bakhita

Feast Day: 8 February

Josephine Bakhita was born in Sudan in around 1869 but was abducted by slave traders at a young age and was so traumatised she forgot her own name. She is known by the cynical name given to her by her abductors - Bakhita, which means "Lucky". Bakhita was passed around from "owner" to "owner" and one of them had her body scarred with intricate patterns. Eventually she ended up with an Italian family who sent her to school with the Canossian sisters in Schio, Venice. There she was baptised Josephine. Contrary to the wishes of the family, she remained with the Canossians and became a religious. She was the doorkeeper of the order and was well loved by the local people for her deep compassion and sweetness which she didn't lose even during the long, painful illness which preceded her death. Josephine Bakhita was canonised in 2000.

First Day: St Josephine, you were taken from your family at an early age and lost your entire identity. We pray for all those children who have been abducted and for their parents and families who suffer not knowing what has become of them. Send your Holy Spirit to comfort them; and may they one day be reunited. We pray especially for [*add your intention*]. *Our Father - Hail Mary - Glory Be*

Second Day: You knew what it was to be a slave, to have no rights, to have lost even your name. We pray for the victims of people traffickers and all those in any kind of slavery. May this evil be wiped out from our world. We pray especially for [*add your intention*]. *Our Father - Hail Mary - Glory Be*

Third Day: St Josephine, one of your owners had your whole body scarred. You knew this terrible pain. We pray for all victims of torture. Help them to heal in body, mind and spirit. May all governments abandon this practice. We pray especially for [*add your intention*]. *Our Father - Hail Mary - Glory Be*

Fourth Day: Even in the terrible suffering of your life, you saw beauty in the world and believed there must be a God because of that beauty. May we too have something of your love for beauty and the natural world. We pray especially for [*add your intention*]. *Our Father - Hail Mary - Glory Be*

Fifth Day: When the family which had rescued you wanted you to leave the Canossians, you had the courage to refuse, even though you were truly grateful to them. Help us to put God's will above all things, even above our natural affections. We pray especially for [*add your intention*]. *Our Father - Hail Mary - Glory Be*

Sixth Day: St Josephine, you were so grateful to know God and to be part of his Church that you often kissed the baptismal font. May we never take for granted the faith we have been offered and give us something of your humility and gratitude for all God does. We pray especially for [*add your intention*]. *Our Father - Hail Mary - Glory Be*

Seventh Day: Your sufferings gave you great compassion for others and you were constantly smiling and always open to those who came to you, no matter how inconvenient it was. St Josephine, may we have something of your sweetness and openness, something of your joy. We pray especially for [*add your intention*]. *Our Father - Hail Mary - Glory Be*

Eighth Day: In your last painful illness you relived your slavery, begging the nurse to loosen your chains. We pray for all those who are weighed down by pain, and we ask that we too may enter the sufferings of our lives where God seems to have abandoned us. May we have the faith to know he has not. We pray especially for [*add your intention*]. *Our Father - Hail Mary - Glory Be*

Ninth Day: Your last words were "Our Lady, Our Lady". May we too know the comfort of the Mother of God, now and at the hour of our death. We pray especially for [*add your intention*]. *Our Father - Hail Mary - Glory Be*

Novena to St Joseph

Feast Day: 19 March, 1 May (St Joseph the Worker)

"Joseph, [Mary's] husband, …was a righteous man" (Matthew 1:19). St Joseph, husband of the Virgin Mary and foster father of Jesus Christ, is one of the best-loved and most powerful intercessors. He is particularly invoked by husbands and fathers, by men in general, by those looking for work, by those with problems at work, and by those looking for somewhere to live. St Joseph is also known as the Protector of the Holy Church, since he was entrusted by God with the care of the Virgin Mary (who is an image of the Church) and the child Jesus. He is also a strong guard against the assaults of the Enemy. Not least, he is the patron of a holy death, and so is often invoked by the dying.

First Day: As husband to Mary and foster-father to Jesus, you are an example of chastity, humility, faithfulness, and obedience to the word of God; intercede for us so that we too may be given these virtues in our lives, and may witness to God's power working in our weakness. We pray especially for [*add your intention*]. *Our Father - Hail Mary - Glory Be*

Second Day: You were chosen by God to be guardian and protector of Jesus and Mary; protect our homes and families; we ask your intercession for husbands and fathers, and for all those who bear responsibility for others. We pray especially for [*add your intention*]. *Our Father - Hail Mary - Glory Be*

Third Day: You know what it is like to have your own plans and expectations overturned by God's plans; help us to trust that he knows better than we do what we really need. We pray especially for [*add your intention*]. *Our Father - Hail Mary - Glory Be*

Fourth Day: You knew what it was like to be exiled from your homeland, to be without a stable place to live; we ask your intercession for those who are looking for somewhere to live, and for those who are far from home. We pray especially for [*add your intention*]. *Our Father - Hail Mary - Glory Be*

Fifth Day: When the child Jesus went missing, and was found in the Temple, you knew the pain of loss, and the joy of finding again; intercede for all who suffer the anguish of separation or bereavement, and help them to know that, like Jesus, we may all be found safe in our Father's house. We pray especially for [*add your intention*]. *Our Father - Hail Mary - Glory Be*

Sixth Day: As you watched over Jesus and Mary on earth, now you are the Protector of the Universal Church; we ask your intercession for all who bear the name of Christian. We pray especially for [*add your intention*]. *Our Father - Hail Mary - Glory Be*

Seventh Day: In the silent witness of your life in Nazareth, the Church sees in you the model of our interior life with Christ; help us to pray, and to put our relationship with Jesus in prayer at the heart of our lives. We pray especially for [*add your intention*]. *Our Father - Hail Mary - Glory Be*

Eighth Day: You know what it is to work; help us to see the dignity and value of the tasks entrusted to us, and to believe that by humbly and faithfully doing what we have to do, we too may give glory to God whether the world recognises us or not. We pray especially for [*add your intention*]. *Our Father - Hail Mary - Glory Be*

Ninth Day: You are the model and patron of Christian death: we ask your intercession for all those who are close to death, and the grace of a holy death for them and for ourselves. We pray especially for [*add your intention*]. *Our Father - Hail Mary - Glory Be*

Novena Prayer to St George

Feast day: 23 April

We all know St George as patron of England, and tamer of dragons. The facts of his life are obscure, but he seems to have been a Roman soldier, probably of the late third century, who was martyred at Lydda in Palestine during the great persecution by the Emperor Diocletian, probably for refusing to renounce Christ and worship the Emperor as a god. His cult was very widespread in the east from that time on; when English soldiers went to the Holy Land on Crusade, they were inspired by this warrior saint; Richard the Lionheart put himself and his army under St George's protection. From then on his popularity in England only grew: Edward III founded the Order of the Garter, with St George as patron, in 1348; Henry V called on St George for aid before the great victory of Agincourt in 1415. Thereafter he was secure as patron of England (although the patronage of two Anglo-Saxon Saint-Kings, Edward the Confessor and Edmund of East Anglia, was not neglected), and his popularity survived the spoliation and wreckage of the Reformation.

Prayer to St George

This prayer to St George can be said for nine days as a novena.

Faithful servant of God and invincible martyr,
St George, inflamed with a burning love of Christ,
you fought against the dragon of pride, falsehood, and
deceit.
Neither pain nor torture,
nor the sword nor death could part you
from the love of Christ.
I implore you for the sake of this love to help me
by your intercession to overcome the temptations that
surround me,
and to bear bravely the trials that oppress me,
so that I may patiently carry my cross,
and let neither distress nor difficulty separate me
from the love of our Lord, Jesus Christ.
Amen.

Novena to St Dymphna

Feast day: 15 May

Tradition says St Dymphna was a seventh century Irish princess, daughter of a Christian mother and a pagan father. Tragically, her mother died when Dymphna was a young teenager and Dymphna's father, the balance of his mind disturbed, tried to marry his own daughter. Dymphna went for help to a priest, Father Gerebran who, understanding that the king, her father, had the power to do whatever he wanted, advised her to flee the country. Fr Gerebran and two others escaped with Dymphna to Gheel in modern-day Belgium. Her father tracked her down however, and when she refused to return with him killed Fr Gerebran and Dymphna, cutting off their heads with his sword. They were buried in tombs by the local people and soon there were reports of the miraculous healing at Dymphna's tomb of the mentally ill and those suffering from epilepsy. More and more mentally ill people came to the shrine and the local people began to look after them in their homes, a tradition which continues today. St Dymphna is patron of those suffering mental illness or epilepsy, and also patron of family harmony.

First Day: St Dymphna, one of your parents was Christian but the other was not and you lived with two different views of the world. We pray for all families which are divided by religion. Intercede for them and bring harmony; help them to live together in love and respect. We pray especially for [*add your intention*]. *Our Father - Hail Mary - Glory Be*

Second Day: You lost your mother when you were a young teenager. We pray for all children who have lost one or both parents through death, divorce or other separation. We ask you to comfort them and help them to experience God's love for them. We pray especially for [*add your intention*]. *Our Father - Hail Mary - Glory Be*

Third Day: Your father was destroyed by grief. We pray for all those who grieve, especially those who do not know the hope of eternal life or those whose grief is affecting their sanity. Intercede for them that they can receive hope and comfort. We pray especially for [*add your intention*]. *Our Father - Hail Mary - Glory Be*

Fourth Day: You had to flee your homeland. We pray for all refugees and those escaping from danger, especially danger in their own families. Intercede that they may find people to help and succour them. We pray especially for [*add your intention*]. *Our Father - Hail Mary - Glory Be*

Fifth Day: You had to run away from home to avoid incest. We pray for all those who have been sexually abused, especially those who have been abused in their own families. We pray for the healing of their self-worth. We pray especially for [*add your intention*]. *Our Father - Hail Mary - Glory Be*

Sixth Day: You are the patron of those with mental illness. We pray for all those who suffer from mental illness and for their families. We pray that they do not lose hope or sight of God. We pray especially for [*add your intention*]. *Our Father - Hail Mary - Glory Be*

Seventh Day: As the sick came to your shrine to be cured, people began to care for and look after them. We pray for all those who work with the mentally ill. We pray that they see in their charges the face of Christ, and always guard their dignity. We pray especially for [*add your intention*]. *Our Father - Hail Mary - Glory Be*

Eighth Day: You lost your mother to death but your father to mental illness and abuse. We pray for all those who have lost their parents to mental illness or addiction, and for all whose parents have treated them badly. Intercede for them that they may be able to forgive. We pray especially for [*add your intention*]. *Our Father - Hail Mary - Glory Be*

Ninth Day: We ask you to intercede for us all, that we might be cured of our delusions and misconceptions whether about ourselves or others. We pray for a healing of our family history. We pray especially for [*add your intention*]. *Our Father - Hail Mary - Glory Be*

Novena to St Anthony of Padua

Feast day: 13 June

St Anthony of Padua was actually born in Portugal, towards the end of the twelfth century. He joined the new order of friars that had recently been founded by St Francis, and moved to Italy. He was a very famous preacher, and was known for his great love for the poor - many churches still collect money for "St Anthony's Bread", for the poor and hungry. He is usually shown with a book, on which the child Jesus is seated. This shows his strong love for Christ as he is present in the proclaimed Word of the Scriptures.

He is very well-known as an intercessor for those who need to find something that has been lost. This apparently stems from a time when one of the friars borrowed his prayer-book without asking, and Anthony appeared to him in a fearsome vision.

Whatever the origin of this, St Anthony is undeniably effective in finding lost items - whether physical objects (anything from car keys upwards) or spiritual things, including faith, hope, and love. The best-known novena to St Anthony is known as the Nine Tuesdays, because it is usually said (as the name suggests) on nine successive Tuesdays; however you could certainly make it on nine consecutive days instead. We give a version of it here.

First Day: Blessed St Anthony, I greet you in the name of the Virgin Mary, Queen of the Angels. I ask you, with her, to bring my request before Almighty God. We pray especially for [*add your intention*]. *Our Father - Hail Mary - Glory Be*

Second Day: Blessed St Anthony, I greet you in the name of the patriarchs and prophets. Like them, you were given the gift of knowledge, even knowledge of the future. I ask you, with them, to bring my request before Almighty God. We pray especially for [*add your intention*]. *Our Father - Hail Mary - Glory Be*

Third Day: Blessed St Anthony, I greet you in the name of all Christ's holy apostles and disciples. God chose you, too, to preach the Gospel and spread the faith. I ask you, with them, to bring my request before Almighty God. We pray especially for [*add your intention*]. *Our Father - Hail Mary - Glory Be*

Fourth Day: Blessed St Anthony, like the martyrs and saints who proclaimed Christ, you were always ready to suffer persecution for his sake. I ask you, with them, to bring my request before Almighty God. We pray especially for [*add your intention*]. *Our Father - Hail Mary - Glory Be*

Fifth Day: Blessed St Anthony, I greet you in the name of all holy bishops and priests. Like them, you were given the grace to convert many to Christ. I ask you, with them, to bring my request before Almighty God. We pray especially for [*add your intention*]. *Our Father - Hail Mary - Glory Be*

Sixth Day: Blessed St Anthony, I greet you and bless God for you, because he gave you the grace to spend your life in good works, like so many holy monks and hermits. You too kept vigil, prayed, fasted, and denied yourself. May your prayers and theirs rise before God on my behalf. We pray especially for [*add your intention*]. *Our Father - Hail Mary - Glory Be*

Seventh Day: Blessed St Anthony, I greet you in the name of all holy virgins and innocents. Like them, you led a life of purity and overcame temptations against it. I ask you, together with them, to pray to God for me. We pray especially for [*add your intention*]. *Our Father - Hail Mary - Glory Be*

Eighth Day: Blessed St Anthony, I greet you in the name of all holy widows, and all holy husbands and wives, and I bless God for all of your virtues. You, like these holy men and women, served God faithfully here on earth; I ask you and them to pray for me now. We pray especially for [*add your intention*]. *Our Father - Hail Mary - Glory Be*

Ninth Day: Blessed St Anthony, I greet you in the name of St Joseph, most chaste husband of the Blessed Virgin Mary. I greet you in the name of all holy men and women now living. I bless the most high God for giving you so much of his love and grace. I ask you, and them, to speak to God for me; may my request be granted if it is for God's greater glory, and for my salvation. We pray especially for [*add your intention*]. *Our Father - Hail Mary - Glory Be*

Novena to St Martha

Feast day: 29 July

St Martha lived with her brother Lazarus and sister Mary in Bethany. Jesus often visited them there. Martha was the one who looked after the house, and is therefore the patron of cooks and homemakers. The Gospels record an incident where Martha complained to Jesus that he had not told her sister Mary to help her with serving their guests, but let her sit and listen to him.

Jesus told Martha not to worry about so many things; and that her sister was right to put listening to him first. Martha later recognised Jesus as the Messiah, and witnessed him raise her brother Lazarus from the dead. After the Resurrection of Jesus, it is said that she and her brother and sister evangelised in France, where Martha converted many people through her preaching, calling them away from the worship of a dragon god.

First Day: Yours was a home that Christ himself was comfortable in. We ask you to help us to be hospitable and open and to make our homes a place where Christ can be present. We pray especially for [*add your intention*]. *Our Father - Hail Mary - Glory Be*

Second Day: You worked hard in your house. Help us to give value to housework and the routine tasks of life. Intercede for us so that we can look after others' needs with serenity and joy. We pray especially for [*add your intention*]. *Our Father - Hail Mary - Glory Be*

Third Day: You served Christ. Help us to serve him in our own lives. We pray especially for [*add your intention*]. *Our Father - Hail Mary - Glory Be*

Fourth Day: Help us to work for the good of others, but always to put Christ first. Help us also to learn from Christ, as you did, not to worry and fret, but to trust in God's all-powerful providence. We pray especially for [*add your intention*]. *Our Father - Hail Mary - Glory Be*

Fifth Day: The Lord rebuked you for your judgement, anger and self-importance and you accepted it. You knew he loved you. We ask that we may be able to accept criticism without remaining resentful and without being destroyed by it. We pray especially for [*add your intention*]. *Our Father - Hail Mary - Glory Be*

Sixth Day: You recognised Jesus as the Christ when he came to your house after your brother's death. Help us to recognise Christ in our lives and to know his love and power. We pray especially for [*add your intention*]. *Our Father - Hail Mary - Glory Be*

Seventh Day: You saw Christ raise your brother from the dead. Intercede for us so our eyes can be opened to the miracles Christ has done in our lives. We pray especially for [*add your intention*]. *Our Father - Hail Mary - Glory Be*

Eighth Day: Christ changed your life. Tradition says that you evangelised in France with your brother and sister. Help us not to be disappointed with our lives but to believe that life can be much more than we ever imagined, in ways we never thought possible. We pray especially for [*add your intention*]. *Our Father - Hail Mary - Glory Be*

Ninth Day: Tradition says you tamed a dragon, turning people away from worshipping a dragon god by your inspired preaching. Help us to see how God can do great things with small people if only we are open to his will. We pray especially for [*add your intention*]. *Our Father - Hail Mary - Glory Be*

Novena to St Maximilian Kolbe

Feast day: 14 August

Maximilian Kolbe was born in 1894 of a Polish mother and ethnic German father. In 1914 his father was hanged by the Russian army after fighting for an independent Poland. As a child, Maximilian had a vision of the Blessed Virgin who offered him the crown of purity or the crown of martyrdom. He chose both. He initially thought of joining the army but instead became a Franciscan priest. He founded a "village" of religious dedicated to Mary Immaculate and a small religious newspaper which became hugely influential in Poland. In 1930 he and four companions went to Japan where they worked for six years. Maximilian suffered poor health all the time he was there but did not think of giving up. Soon after his return to Poland, the country was invaded by the Nazis and he was arrested, and was eventually sent to Auschwitz. He ministered to his fellow prisoners before finally offering his life in exchange for that of a married man who was one of ten prisoners sentenced to be locked up and left to starve to death. Fr Maximilian encouraged the other prisoners in his death cell, and announced the Gospel even as they all starved to death. Finally only he was left alive and was murdered by lethal injection, accepting death with peace.

First Day: When still a child you entrusted your future to the Mother of God and accepted the crowns of purity and martyrdom. Help us to learn to be generous with our lives in the service of God. We pray especially for [*add your intention*]. *Our Father - Hail Mary - Glory Be*

Second Day: You had a great love of the military and thought of joining the army but instead began the Militia Immaculatae to work for the conversion of sinners. We remember all those who serve in the armed forces and their families. We pray especially for [*add your intention*]. *Our Father - Hail Mary - Glory Be*

Third Day: You began a small religious newspaper which led to an upsurge of faith amongst your countrymen. May we too realise that nothing we do is too small for God to use. We pray especially for [*add your intention*]. *Our Father - Hail Mary - Glory Be*

Fourth Day: You had such zeal for the proclamation of the Gospel that you went to Japan with no money and no word of the language and what you built is now the centre of the Franciscan province there. May we share in your zeal to announce the Good News through our words and our lives. We pray especially for [*add your intention*]. *Our Father - Hail Mary - Glory Be*

Fifth Day: When the Nazis had invaded your country and you were under suspicion you said, "No one in the world can change truth". May we hold firm to the one who is the Truth, Jesus Christ. We pray especially for [*add your intention*]. *Our Father - Hail Mary - Glory Be*

Sixth Day: In prison you were asked whether you believed in Christ and were beaten every time you said you did. You persevered in your witness. May we still hold fast to Christ even in suffering or pain, and if we are persecuted for that belief may we have the courage not to desert him. We pray especially for [*add your intention*]. *Our Father - Hail Mary - Glory Be*

Seventh Day: Even when you were sent to Auschwitz you did not abandon your vocation as priest. Although you were beaten almost to death you still heard confessions and spoke of Christ's love. We ask you to give us something of your conviction and courage in front of the sufferings of our lives. We pray especially for [*add your intention*]. *Our Father - Hail Mary - Glory Be*

Eighth Day: When a fellow prisoner was sentenced to death by starvation you volunteered to take his place: to die so that he had a chance of life. May we always remember the words of Our Lord, "he who loses his life for my sake will find it" and give us the courage to lose our lives in whatever way is asked of us. We pray especially for [*add your intention*]. *Our Father - Hail Mary - Glory Be*

Ninth Day: Because you were killed by an injection of carbolic acid, you are the patron of drug users. We pray for all those who suffer this terrible addiction and for their families. May they have the courage and help they need to turn their lives around. We pray especially for [*add your intention*]. *Our Father - Hail Mary - Glory Be*

Novena to St Joseph of Cupertino

Feast day: 18 September

Because his father had died leaving debts and his family was consequently homeless, Joseph Desa was an unwelcome addition when he was born in Cupertino, Italy in 1603. As a child he was slow witted and had a habit of standing with his mouth open staring into space. He also had a terrible temper, probably born of frustration. Even his own mother thought him worthless. As a young man he joined the Capuchins but was sent away because the ecstasies he experienced made him unsuitable for work. Finally he was accepted by the Franciscans who, seeing his holiness, put him forward to train for the priesthood. Joseph was so unintelligent that the best he could do was to study a small portion of the material he was supposed to know, and then pray that that's what he would be asked. Whilst with the Franciscans he began to levitate in ecstasy at the mention of any holy thing and only a command from his superior could bring him to earth. Joseph was investigated (and exonerated) by the Inquisition because of his antigravitational activities. This also caused his superiors to move him into seclusion. He had his own room and chapel and was unable to leave them. Often those in charge even forgot to bring him food but he accepted everything with humility. He died a holy death aged sixty. He is a patron of students doing exams and of air travellers.

First Day: You were an unwanted child and were thought worthless even by your own mother. Intercede for all unwanted children that they may come to know they were born out of God's love for them. We pray especially for [*add your intention*]. *Our Father - Hail Mary - Glory Be*

Second Day: You were an angry, frustrated child. We pray for all who struggle to express themselves, and that you help us overcome sins of anger. We pray especially for [*add your intention*]. *Our Father - Hail Mary - Glory Be*

Third Day: You experienced no love in your family and were considered of little account by all who knew you. We pray for all who have experienced the same. May we learn to treat everyone as having the worth they have in God's eyes. We pray especially for [*add your intention*]. *Our Father - Hail Mary - Glory Be*

Fourth Day: You suffered because of your lack of intelligence. We pray for all those who struggle at school. May they take comfort from the fact that lack of intelligence didn't stop you becoming a saint. We pray especially for [*add your intention*]. *Our Father - Hail Mary - Glory Be*

Fifth Day: You did the best with the little intelligence you had, and put the rest in God's hands. That way you passed all your exams and became a priest. We pray for all those struggling with exams. May we also do our best in everything and trust in God to guide our lives. We pray especially for [*add your intention*]. *Our Father - Hail Mary - Glory Be*

Sixth Day: Even the thought or mention of anything holy made you levitate in ecstasy. Grant us something of the understanding and reverence for God and his saints that you had. We pray especially for [*add your intention*]. *Our Father - Hail Mary - Glory Be*

Seventh Day: Only when your superior ordered you to, were you able to come back down to earth. May we too have a love for and obedience to the teachings of the Church. We pray especially for [*add your intention*]. *Our Father - Hail Mary - Glory Be*

Eighth Day: You were unjustly suspected, investigated, confined to your room and neglected by those charged with looking after you. You accepted all this with humility. We pray for all those unjustly imprisoned, and that we too may have the humility to accept injustice for the love of Christ. We pray especially for [*add your intention*]. *Our Father - Hail Mary - Glory Be*

Ninth Day: Because you could levitate you are the patron of air travellers. We pray for all those travelling by plane that they may safely reach their destinations. We pray especially for [*add your intention*]. *Our Father - Hail Mary - Glory Be*

Novena to St Jude

Feast day: 28 October

The apostle St Jude takes only a modest role in the Gospel narratives, but he is probably the best-known intercessor of all the Twelve. According to tradition, St Jude, together with his companion the apostle St Simon (not Simon Peter, but Simon the Zealot) who may have been his brother, preached the Gospel in various parts of the middle east (Persia, Mesopotamia, Armenia, and around the Black Sea) and were eventually martyred in Georgia.

For some reason, St Jude has become known as the saint of lost causes, or of things despaired of: someone whose intercession is especially powerful in cases where all hope seems gone. Whatever the reason for this, many people can testify to the strength of his prayers for them.

First Day: O blessed apostle, St Jude, who laboured among the peoples of many lands and performed miracles in despairing cases, I ask you to take an interest in my need. You understand me. Hear my prayer, and plead for me. May I be patient in learning God's will and courageous in carrying it out. We pray especially for [*add your intention*]. *Our Father - Hail Mary - Glory Be*

Second Day: O blessed apostle, St Jude, grant that I may always serve the Lord as he deserves to be served, and live as he wants me to live. I ask you to intercede for me. May I be enlightened as to what is best for me now, and not forget the blessings I have received in the past. We pray especially for [*add your intention*]. *Our Father - Hail Mary - Glory Be*

Third Day: Holy St Jude, who so faithfully helped to spread the Gospel, I ask you to remember me and my needs. May the Lord listen to your prayers on my behalf. May I always pray with fervour and devotion, resigning myself to God's will, and seeing his purposes in all my trials. Help me to know that God will not leave any sincere prayer unanswered. We pray especially for [*add your intention*]. *Our Father - Hail Mary - Glory Be*

Fourth Day: St Jude, you were called as one of the Apostles. Listen with compassion as I ask for your help; pray that God may answer my prayer as he knows best, giving me grace to see his purpose in all things. We pray especially for [*add your intention*]. *Our Father - Hail Mary - Glory Be*

Fifth Day: Holy St Jude, apostle and companion of Jesus Christ, your life was filled with zeal for the Gospel. Listen to my prayers now. May I never forget the blessings I have received in the past, and may I be resigned to God's holy will. We pray especially for [*add your intention*]. *Our Father - Hail Mary - Glory Be*

Sixth Day: St Jude, apostle of Christ and helper in desperate cases, listen to my prayer. May I seek only what pleases God and is best for my salvation. May what I desire be granted, if it is for my good; help me to know that God leaves no prayer without an answer, even if it is not what I may expect. We pray especially for [*add your intention*]. *Our Father - Hail Mary - Glory Be*

Seventh Day: Holy apostle, St Jude, Christ chose you as one of the Twelve, and you were given the gift of martyrdom. I know you are close to God. Listen to my request; and help me to see God's purpose in all things. We pray especially for [*add your intention*]. *Our Father - Hail Mary - Glory Be*

Eighth Day: Holy St Jude, pray that I may always imitate Christ and live according to his will. Intercede for me, that I may obtain whatever I need for my salvation. Help me to accept from God whatever answer he gives to what I now ask. We pray especially for [*add your intention*]. *Our Father - Hail Mary - Glory Be*

Ninth Day: Holy St Jude, apostle and martyr, help my life be pleasing to God. Intercede for me today; pray especially that I may seek God's will above all things, and see his love for me in whatever trials or difficulties he sends me. We pray especially for [*add your intention*]. *Our Father - Hail Mary - Glory Be*

Novena to St Martin de Porres

Feast day: 3 November

Martin was born in Peru in 1579, the illegitimate son of a Spanish father and a mother who was a freed slave. Rejected by his father for being too black, he grew up in poverty with his mother and sister. From an early age he had a great love of God and of the poor. He became a Dominican lay brother as he could not be accepted into the order because of his colour. He worked in menial jobs and then as an infirmarian. He became renowned for his medical ability but he eschewed the fame that came with that and remained humble and hidden. He was also known for his love of the poor and also of animals, especially dogs. He was canonised in 1962 and is the patron of interracial harmony.

First Day: You were rejected and abandoned by your father. We pray for all those who experience that same situation and for all those who are rejected for not meeting their family's expectations in some way. May they be reconciled, as you were finally reconciled with your own father. We pray especially for [*add your intention*]. *Our Father - Hail Mary - Glory Be*

Second Day: As a child your mother was your only parent. We pray for all single parent families, and ask that you help them in the particular difficulties that they face. We pray especially for [*add your intention*]. *Our Father - Hail Mary - Glory Be*

Third Day: You grew up poor but you always gave to those who had even less. We ask you to help us to become generous with our goods and our time, never feeling that we have nothing to offer. We pray especially for [*add your intention*]. *Our Father - Hail Mary - Glory Be*

Fourth Day: When you were eight your father reappeared and whisked you off to a prosperous life in another country before sending you back to the life you had before. We pray for all those whose family life is insecure and disrupted. May they experience, as you did, that God is their security. We pray especially for [*add your intention*]. *Our Father - Hail Mary - Glory Be*

Fifth Day: You lived alone working to support yourself from a very young age. We pray for all children who have adult responsibilities; for all children who support their families; and for all children who are carers for their parents. Intercede for them that they may receive the help they need. We pray especially for [*add your intention*]. *Our Father - Hail Mary - Glory Be*

Sixth Day: You were rejected because of your colour - even by the Church. We pray for all those who suffer discrimination of any kind. May all in authority deal with everyone justly, and may we treat each other as brothers and sisters in Christ. We pray especially for [*add your intention*]. *Our Father - Hail Mary - Glory Be*

Seventh Day: You were not ashamed to do the most menial of jobs. You were even happy cleaning lavatories. May we too learn humility and come to see that all work can be holy. We pray especially for [*add your intention*]. *Our Father - Hail Mary - Glory Be*

Eighth Day: You were known for your love of animals. Help us to love and respect all God's creation. We pray especially for [*add your intention*]. *Our Father - Hail Mary - Glory Be*

Ninth Day: You had great medical skill and love for other people. We pray for all who are involved in caring for the sick. May they share something of your compassion and your skill. We pray especially for [*add your intention*]. *Our Father - Hail Mary - Glory Be*

Novena to Blessed Charles de Foucauld

Feast day: 1 December

As a young man, Charles de Foucauld was rich and privileged. He ran through a small fortune on high living and mistresses, and sought adventure in the army and in exotic travel. Eventually, God touched his heart, and he gave up his old life to enter a monastery. But this was not enough for him; he returned to the deserts of North Africa, where as a young soldier he had been impressed by the religious devotion of the Muslim tribesmen, and lived amongst them as a hermit, witnessing to Christ without words, but simply by his way of life. He was shot to death by robbers in 1916, when after fifteen years in the desert he had made only one convert. But, despite appearances, his life and witness was not in vain: after his death, his example has brought many to God, and inspires the "Little Brothers and Sisters of Jesus", who follow Charles's example by living in "the lowest place", and seek to bring God's love to others in a silent and hidden way.

First Day: You knew what it is like to be burdened by many sins. Help us not to despair in the face of our sins, especially our habitual sins, but really to believe in God's power to change us. We pray especially for [*add your intention*]. *Our Father - Hail Mary - Glory Be*

Second Day: You turned to God, and knew his mercy on your sins. Help us to hear his call to repent the evil we have done, and to welcome the grace to return to our loving Father as you did. We pray especially for [*add your intention*]. *Our Father - Hail Mary - Glory Be*

Third Day: You heard God's to follow him in a particular way. Help us, too, to hear God's call to us to love him and our neighbour in the vocation he has planned for us. We pray especially for [*add your intention*]. *Our Father - Hail Mary - Glory Be*

Fourth Day: You lived amongst strangers, and saw God's hand at work in them. Help us to find God wherever we are, especially in the places we might not think to look for him. We pray especially for [*add your intention*]. *Our Father - Hail Mary - Glory Be*

Fifth Day: You lived in the desert, and found God in solitude and silence. Help us to make space for God in our lives. We pray especially for [*add your intention*]. *Our Father - Hail Mary - Glory Be*

Sixth Day: You gave witness to God most of all by what you did, rather than by what you said. Pray for us, that we too may be a sign of God's love to those around us, more by how we live than by what we say. We pray especially for [*add your intention*]. *Our Father - Hail Mary - Glory Be*

Seventh Day: Your mission seemed to be a failure, and your life's work to have come to nothing, yet you did not give up. Help us to persevere in doing God's will, even if - especially if - we can see only failure and defeat: help us to know that, in God's sight, the only important thing is to do his will in love, and to live in hope, not discouragement. We pray especially for [*add your intention*]. *Our Father - Hail Mary - Glory Be*

Eighth Day: You abandoned your whole life to God's will. Pray for us, that we may have something of the faith you had. We pray especially for [*add your intention*]. *Our Father - Hail Mary - Glory Be*

Ninth Day: You loved God until the end, and even in your death you praised him. Intercede for us, that death may find us blessing God for all his mercies. We pray especially for [*add your intention*]. *Our Father - Hail Mary - Glory Be*

LIVING LIFE
TO THE FULL

What's the Point?

Being happy

*B*lessed are the poor in spirit, for theirs is the kingdom of heaven. Blessed are those who mourn, for they shall be comforted. Blessed are the meek, for they shall inherit the earth. Blessed are those who hunger and thirst for justice, for they shall be satisfied. (Matthew 5:3-6)*

We did not choose to exist; we find ourselves already existing amid a network of relationships and in the middle of a world we did not make. As we grow up, we "come to ourselves" and find that we must live our own lives and make many decisions *for ourselves*. We have to decide what to *do*. Sometimes we just act out of habit, or do what everyone else is doing. At other times we are faced with conscious choices: little choices, such as what to cook for supper, or what to buy for someone as a present; big choices, such as whether to abandon a job in the hope of something better, or whether a certain person is the right one to marry. The ability to decide things for ourselves is one of the things that mark human beings out from other animals. The Bible puts it in this way: "It was the Lord who made human beings in the beginning, and he has left them in the hands of their own counsel." (*Sirach* 15:14)

But before we make a choice about something, we first have to be clear about *why* we are doing it: what is it that we are trying to achieve? What is the aim or purpose of our action? - I get the bus to go shopping. I go shopping to buy food. I buy food to eat. And why do I eat? I eat to stay alive: but eating is also a pleasure, a relaxation, and (normally) a social occasion. It is an important part of

human life. But this brings us back further. What is it that makes sense of our whole life? What is it that we are **seeking** in and through all our various activities? What is it ultimately **all about?**

The answer to this question is happiness - or, perhaps better - **blessedness** or **human flourishing**. "Happiness" in this sense means the **true end** of human life taken as a whole. Different people may organise their lives around different things. There are some people who organise their lives around food, those "whose God is their belly" as St Paul puts it. Some people may not find any one thing that makes sense of their lives: but everyone realises that - wherever it is to be found - it is a good thing to find true happiness, and to find meaning in one's life.

The *ultimate* source of this meaning to human life is whatever principle or being it is that directs the whole universe, and gives life and shape to the natural world and to human history. If there *is* a meaning to life, then this meaning has to come from the Source of all life - and this is what Christians call the mystery of God. Those who believe in God can have confidence that human life *does* make sense, and that it *can* find fulfilment. The danger for those who do not explicitly believe in God is not so much that they will believe in *nothing* (for this requires a remarkable, if not perverse, kind of strength), but rather that they will believe in *anything*. A decline in traditional religion leads most people *not* into atheism, but into esoteric or "alternative" cults and superstitions - which might give some degree of meaning to life. Otherwise they will be led into diversions, such as entertainment or recreational drugs - which might distract them from the lack of meaning in their lives.

The true happiness that we are all searching for will sometimes involve suffering or the willingness to suffer. The happiness we seek will not always be immediate, and it will not always be obvious. For instance, friendship, which is a part of happiness - and an image of our ultimate happiness in God - can sometimes be a cause of pain, even though of itself it gives pleasure. It is only through doing the right thing that we will become truly "happy", in the sense of *being all that we can be*: flourishing and finding fulfilment as human beings - being *blessed*. If, on the road to happiness, we sometimes have to *suffer* something bad instead of *doing* something bad, this is never because we love suffering for its own sake. We may, for example, have to make an act of self-sacrifice; but this is always for our own good or the good of others.

Suffering is sometimes a means, but it can never be an end, for our final hope is to find happiness, with others and for others, in God who is the source of all meaning and all life. We are moved to happiness by a desiring-love, but we *find* happiness in a friendship-love, a love that comes from God. As a general principle, then, doing the right thing in our lives involves seeking happiness through *loving most strongly that which is most loveable*. It is because of this love that, despite their many sufferings, the saints are the happiest of people, for they live blessed, full and meaningful lives.

Objective Right and Wrong

And Jesus said to him, "Why do you ask me about what is good? There is only One who is good. If you would enter life, keep the commandments." He said to him, "Which?" And Jesus said, "You shall not kill, You shall not commit adultery, You shall not steal, You shall not bear false witness, Honour your father and mother; and, You shall love your neighbour as yourself." (Matthew 19:17-19)

In matters of science, beliefs can be true or false, and theories can be more or less adequate. People may argue about matters of fact, but they are often able to find some way of testing who is right and who is wrong. Moral issues seem different. Arguments about abortion or animal experimentation, euthanasia or homosexuality, rarely convince anyone who was not previously convinced. As a result, many people think that value judgements are not about "objective" reality - that is to say, they cannot be either "true" or "false". Rather, they are thought of merely as expressions of emotion, or matters of taste (what someone happens to like or dislike). Furthermore, we know more nowadays about cultures that have very different customs from our own. Why should we be in a better position to judge than people in these cultures? How can we say that others are wrong?

Of course, it is easy to misunderstand another **culture**, and to assume that we have something to teach it but nothing to learn from it. It can be hard work to become familiar with the language, lifestyle and customs of others. Nevertheless, it can be done - and there are many books, articles and novels that give an accurate sense of other cultures. Indeed, we are able to come to understand other cultures *precisely* because of the many things that we all share as human beings - the importance of friendship and family, ideas of loyalty and betrayal, the experience of sickness and death, of joy and feasting. For example, although the *ways* people grieve are shaped by their cultures and their own personal histories, the need to *grieve* is universal. Once we recognise and are sensitive to such cultural differences, then we can become aware of the deeper universal similarities. Common moral judgements are *thus* possible, because we all share a common humanity.

When we learn to speak, it is in one particular **language**; but once we have learned it, we are able to understand truths that are common and universal. In a similar way, we learn what it is to be human by growing up within a specific human community with its own particular culture - but through this community we come to appreciate human values that are universal. This wider awareness enables us to identify and criticise practices within our own culture, or to compare our culture to other cultures. The abolition of slavery, for example, came about because people were not trapped within their own culture. Slavery's opponents were able to appeal to the transcendent value of human freedom, and so to criticise local prejudices and argue for a better way of doing things.

Some basic understanding of right and wrong is common to all mature human beings, and is what the Catholic tradition calls the **Natural Law**; it is in this sense that Catholics understand the following words of St Paul:

"When Pagans, who do not have the Law, do by nature what the Law requires, they show that what the Law requires is written on their hearts." (*Romans* 2:14-15)

Of course, while almost everyone agrees about the basic principles of human action, the closer we get to particular actions, the more room there is for disagreement. Although moral judgements may be either true or false, they are not always *obvious* or self-evident. The arguments sometimes need to be very subtle, and the feelings they arouse can be powerful. People are often unwilling to change their own way of life, and can become attached to doing something that is wrong simply because it is pleasant or convenient. Hence moral debates are often over-emotional. All customs and actions need to be judged by the measure of the Natural Law, which can be discovered by reasoned reflection on the meaning of human life.

The Bible teaches us many new things about the moral life, concerning forgiveness and the friendship of God (see further below). However, at the same time it reminds us of those basic universal truths that, in principle, we could discover for ourselves, but for which we need a reliable guide. Framing these truths in terms of a few fundamental rules helps remind us during times of weakness and temptation of what we deeply believe to be true, but can easily fool ourselves into neglecting. These truths are present in the Law that God gave to Moses, especially in the heart of that Law, the **Ten Commandments**:

1. Do not worship false gods.
2. Do not abuse the name of God.
3. Keep the Sabbath day as a holy day.
4. Honour your father and your mother.
5. Do not kill.
6. Do not commit adultery.
7. Do not steal.
8. Do not lie.
9. Do not desire to possess your neighbour's wife.
10. Do not desire to possess anything that belongs to your neighbour.

(Exodus 20:2-17; *Deuteronomy* 5:6-21)

Not Just Following Rules

*A*nd *Jesus said to them. "Have you never read what David did when he was in need and was hungry, he and those who were with him: how he entered the house of God, when Abiathar was high priest, and ate the bread of the Presence, which it is not lawful for any but the priests to eat, and also gave it to those who were with him?" And he said to them, "The Sabbath was made for man, not man for the Sabbath".* (Mark 2:25-27)

There are some actions and customs that distort or destroy that which is good and valuable in human life. That is why we need **rules** like the Ten Commandments - to stop us from doing harm to others and to ourselves. However, rules on their own are not sufficient. How do we know if the rule applies? Is there a rule that tells us when *every* rule applies?

And how do we know when to apply *this* rule? Even with negative rules like "Do not steal" it is not always obvious what *counts* as stealing. What happens when someone is in great need - for instance, in an emergency? What about borrowing and not returning? If a deal is unfair must it still be honoured? There are many fringe cases where it takes a wise and experienced person to judge whether a particular case is an example of stealing, and therefore forbidden by the commandment.

If this is true of the negative rules, then it is even truer of the positive commandments. "Honour your father and your mother". But how? When? To what extent? Does this rule mean that children must always obey their parents? If not, what are the exceptions? There cannot be a rule for every one of these questions. So rules are not enough on their own: they need a person who has an understanding of what the rules are for, what values they protect, and when they apply.

Furthermore, if we are to do the right thing, then we need more than simply an understanding of what is at stake. We must also be **good people**. An ungrateful son might refuse to go to a family event, in order to dishonour his mother and father, perhaps because he wants to make a show of his independence. Likewise, someone might steal while knowing full well that this action would cause great suffering; they might regret the fact, but be too greedy to return what was stolen. Another person might want very much to do the right thing, and see the attraction of doing it, but be too frightened of the consequences.

In order to do the right thing in a given situation it is not enough to know the rules; we need good dispositions of character or **virtues** - a concept the Christian tradition adopted from the ancient Greek philosophers. We need *practical wisdom*, so as to know what values are at stake, and what rules apply. We need to be *just* and fair-minded so that we are inclined to give people their due. Finally, we need to be brave in the face of danger, and *temperate* in the face of desire, so that fear or desire do not prevent us from doing the right thing. These four virtues - Practical Wisdom (also known as "Prudence"), Justice, Courage and Temperance - are called the **"cardinal" virtues** (from a Latin word, *cardo*, which means "hinge"). They are the hinges on which good character hangs.

Rules and virtues work together: a virtuous person will understand the true meaning of the rules and be able to apply them. Virtues are like the skills of a musician or an athlete: they can be cultivated by practice and hard work, and become a sort of second nature, enabling the person who has them to perform well. On the other hand, virtues differ from skills in that skills make for a good *performance* whereas virtues make for a good *person* (it is possible to be a good performer without being a good person: a "virtuoso" on the violin might be a person bereft of moral goodness).

In the end, it is only the virtuous person who is good - the one who is wise, just, courageous, and temperate. Some people are not virtuous simply because they are immature, and have not yet developed their character. This is commonly true of young people, but it is also true of older people who have not taken sufficient responsibility for their own lives. At the other extreme, it is possible to have a stable and developed character, but one that is disposed towards a *distorted* or *corrupted* vision of the good life. This is much worse than simply being ignorant or immature. Bad dispositions of character, formed by deliberate acts, are called vices. The virtues act together in harmony, but the vices pull in different directions: you can be bad through being too assertive, or by not being assertive enough. A list can be made of the various vices that are opposed to the cardinal virtues - folly or cunning, injustice or self-destructiveness, cowardice or rashness, greediness or puritanism. However, the most famous list of vices in the Christian tradition is the **Seven Deadly Sins**: Pride, Envy, Anger, Apathy (Sloth), Avarice, Gluttony and Lust.

Friendship with God

Greater love has no man than this: that he lay down his life for his friends. You are my friends if you do what I command you. No longer do I call you servants for the servant does not know what his master is doing; but I have called you friends, for all that I have heard from my Father I have made known to you. (John 15:13-15)

What has been said so far - about happiness, natural law and the virtues - is only the beginning. We have not yet reached the heart of the Gospel message; for no purely *natural* account of human life be sufficient to capture the true destiny of human beings. Even the deepest and most important elements of human life - married love, friendship, the search for wisdom - are not the end.

For human beings have a capacity and a **destiny** which exceeds any created source of fulfilment. We were each made "in the image of God" and our ultimate happiness lies in nothing less than finding peace in God. St Augustine once wrote: "You made us for yourself, O Lord, and our hearts are restless until they rest in you."

Furthermore, even natural justice is difficult for us to maintain on our own: even the best systems of justice are not free from corruption, and indeed in many countries corruption is not even recognised. Every nation has its underside, its forgotten past or hidden present: blood money, slave trading, questionable wars fought for dubious motives, the unjust torture or imprisonment of dissenters. Every nation has its "haves" and its "have-nots".

Every nation knows its selfishness, deception and political intrigue. However, one cannot trace this back to poor education and ignorance alone. There is something *disordered* within each one of us: a weakness and a flaw that we cannot fix on our own. This is due to an alienation from God - a state that we exist in from the moment we are conceived. This is what Christians call **original sin**.

So we have a double need: only God can give us a share in the Life that will bring us perfect happiness, and only God can bring order to the disorder within us. This double need was shown to us by the coming of Jesus, our Saviour. Jesus preached mercy, healed people who were sick or troubled by evil spirits, and forgave sins. When he was executed, it was the clearest sign of how deeply sick the world is. The chief priests, the Roman governor, the people of the city, even one of his own disciples, all conspired to arrest, torture and murder him, though he was innocent of any crime. Jesus was "dangerous" because he could not be tamed or manipulated. He showed the fierce mercy of God.

When Jesus rose from the dead, this showed that God the Father accepted the gift of his Son's life, as the basis for a **New Covenant** with mankind to answer this double need. Jesus in turn promised the Holy Spirit would come, to be the giver of new life for his disciples. The help we need from God is God himself - the Holy Spirit, given to inspire us and make us new. We call the presence of the Holy Spirit in us "grace", a word that means "free gift". The Christian life, then, is not just a life of law and virtue in pursuit of happiness; it is also a *friendship with God*. It may be objected that friendship is only truly possible between equals, and that no one can be equal with God. However, the message of the Gospel is that, in Jesus, God *humbled himself* and became human, like us, so that we could have a share in his own life and, therefore, a sort of equality, by being his "adopted" sons and daughters. In this way we can now have a new dignity and freedom as God's own children.

The moral life of the Christian, then, is not only about education in virtue. It is also a *drama* of sin and the grace of God. We have been rescued by God from the trouble we have brought upon ourselves by original sin, by the sins of the world and by our own personal sins, and have been given a new way of life. That is why pride and an unforgiving attitude are so dangerous for the Christian: pride stops us from recognising our own need; a failure to forgive others (or to ask for their forgiveness when we need to) cuts us off from the mercy that God wishes to show us also.

Our help comes from God, not from ourselves. Mercy is shown to us; we must show mercy to others. Jesus himself taught us to pray, "Forgive us our trespasses, as we forgive those who trespass against us" (*Matthew* 6:12). If we act otherwise, then we resist or reject the friendship of God. This new way of life, bestowed on us by God in the Sacrament of Baptism, brings with it those special virtues that give the Christian life its very shape. First comes *faith*, the gift that enables us to believe what God has revealed.

Next comes *hope*, by which we entrust our lives to God. Finally, and most importantly, comes *love* - love for God and for others. These virtues, which make us not only good but *holy*, are called the **Theological Virtues** (see *1 Corinthians* 13). Along with these inspired virtues, God also gives particular gifts to make us responsive to the promptings of the Holy Spirit within us. The Church lists seven such **Gifts of the Holy Spirit**: Wisdom, Understanding, Counsel, Courage, Knowledge, Piety and Fear of the Lord (*Isaiah* 11:2).

How to Decide

If it feels right, do it?

The eye is the lamp of the body. So, if your eye is sound, your whole body will be full of light: but if your eye is not sound, your whole body will be full of darkness. If then the light in you is darkness, how great is the darkness! (*Matthew* 6:22-23)

It is part of the dignity of being human that we have the **freedom** to decide for ourselves how to act. Rather than limiting our freedom, the Gospel and the Holy Spirit actually *enable* it; they bring us a new and deeper freedom which allows us to liberate ourselves from the misery of sin. Natural law, the cardinal and theological virtues, and the gifts of the Holy Spirit provide a wide scope of action for us. There are many things we *might* do, countless ways to live out the Christian life. Not every way of life will be open to us; but the options are nearly always wider than we think, and it remains for us to take one particular path.

The dignity of human and Christian freedom is something that must always be respected. A person can help someone make a decision through support, advice or example, but that person cannot make up their mind for them. All of us must learn to take responsibility for our own decisions and make them as best we can.

Conscience is our considered *judgement* about whether a particular action, committed or merely contemplated, is good or bad. It is never right to act against our conscience for reasons of weakness or cowardice; nor is it proper to encourage others to act against theirs. "It is right not to do anything that makes your brother stumble" (*Romans* 14:21).

In this sense the judgement of conscience must always be respected. But our conscience can also get things wrong. Just because I myself judge that this particular action ought to be done (or avoided) here and now, it does not follow that I have necessarily made the right decision. Our judgements about what to do must be informed by the virtue of prudence (practical wisdom), by self-knowledge and knowledge of the circumstances, by seeking advice and by being open to correction. If someone tries hard to make the right decision, but gets it wrong, then the mistake might well be innocent: a good person will sometimes do bad things out of ignorance. But *some* ignorance results from our own ill will. People who make a habit of taking advantage of others, for example, will soon stop feeling pangs of conscience for doing so. Their view of right and wrong will become darkened, and it will become more difficult for them to see things clearly. When this happens, ignorance is no longer a legitimate excuse.

Although merely doing what feels right *may* be the right thing to do, we should always think through the implications and the consequences of our actions. Sometimes it will be important to overcome our initial feelings. Acting without thought and without shame is not a sign of strength, but a sign of weakness, laziness or cowardice. Furthermore, if we are given responsibility over others, we must sometimes *discipline* them regardless of their willingness to accept this. For instance, a worker who causes offence by telling racist jokes should be reprimanded, not just for his own sake, but also for the sake of his colleagues, and for the common good. The Gospel tells us that correction among equals - colleagues, co-workers, classmates - is also a responsibility; but such fraternal correction will be effective only if the person corrected is willing to accept *criticism* - so we ought to think carefully about when and how to approach that person. If it seems unlikely that a person will change, then we should weigh the value of trying to correct them against the trouble it might cause. However, if someone comes to us looking for approval which we cannot give, then we must overcome our cowardice or embarrassment and say what needs to be said. Fraternal correction, when it is done well, is an act of love.

Tough Decisions

Then Jesus said to them, "My soul is very sorrowful, even to death; remain here, and watch with me." And going a little farther he fell on his face and prayed, "My Father; if it be possible, let this cup pass from me; nevertheless, not as I will, but as thou wilt." (Matthew 26:38-39)

The Christian life, inspired by the Holy Spirit, is not just about *occasional* difficult choices. It is about the attitude or spirit behind *all* our acts, great and small. However, in this life we walk by faith rather than by sight, and there are many things we do not understand. We are sometimes faced with difficult decisions and find ourselves at a loss as to what we should do.

Decisions may be difficult for different reasons. First there are decisions that are *intellectually* difficult. We must have the courage to act on our limited knowledge, for inactivity is a decision in itself. We must act as best we can and leave it to God to bring good from our mistakes. We cannot be expected to see things as God sees them. Other decisions are *emotionally* difficult; we have to face the prospect of suffering, or resist the attraction of immediate pleasures. These difficulties are just as real as those of moral quandaries. Finally, there are many decisions that are difficult in *both* ways: they are perplexing *and* emotionally difficult.

The difficulty of telling someone that their loved one has died is, in part, a matter of knowing what to say; but it is mainly the difficulty of sharing emotional distress. We can grapple with these difficulties, but they do not always have a "perfect" solution that will make everyone happy. Thus they give rise to the temptation to accept a false solution that *appears* to make everything "all right", if only we are willing to do some little act of wickedness.

This false promise has even been codified into a system called **proportionalism**, by which *any* act can be allowed if there is a "proportionate reason" for doing it, that is, a strong enough motive. "Proportionalism" is a system that is incompatible with the Church's tradition. It was condemned by Pope St John Paul II in 1993, in an "encyclical" - a letter to the whole Church - called *Veritatis Splendor* ('The Splendour of Truth'). There are certain actions we must exclude *altogether* because they are things that a virtuous person would never do: betray the faith; lie; murder; steal; commit adultery. The Catholic Church calls such actions *intrinsically bad*, and says that it is always wrong to do evil in order that good may come of it (*Romans* 3:8). Sometimes we are faced with a dilemma in which whatever we do, someone will be harmed. In such situations we should be guided by the principle of double effect: side effects should be assessed differently from effects we aim to bring about. Adopting the lesser of two evils is a principle which applies only to weighing side effects - where what we are intending, as an end or means, is not in itself morally wrong.

For example, in the case of an "ectopic pregnancy" - when the embryo has implanted in the wrong place and the mother's life is threatened - the doctor may not respond with a deliberate attack on the child. However, the doctor may remove the damaged organ from the woman, even if the doctor knows that, as a side effect, the child will die. Causing death *unintentionally* is very serious, but may be permitted in certain extreme circumstances. Murder - the deliberate and *intended* killing of the innocent, on mere human authority - is never justified, no matter how extreme the situation. It matters crucially whether the effect is "direct" or "indirect"; that is, intended or unintended.

Many moral dilemmas involve **co-operation** with evil. Co-operation in common projects is an important social virtue, but it poses a problem when we find ourselves involved in someone else's wrongdoing. Should a doctor do the paperwork for a woman who is going to have an abortion? Should a company trade with an oppressive and unjust government? Should a newspaper print letters expressing intolerant or inflammatory views? Acting in such a way that you share another person's wrongful aims is called *direct* or *formal* co-operation, and is always wrong. Doing what in effect helps the person, but without sharing his or her wrongful aims, is called *indirect* or *material* co-operation, and this need not be immoral.

However, material co-operation should be avoided where this is possible without doing harm, especially where the co-operation may be a cause of scandal, and non-co-operation can be an important "prophetic" witness, calling attention to an ongoing injustice. Morality is not, however, only about *excluding* certain actions; we must above all try to do something *positive*. Following rules is not enough on its own to tell us what particular positive thing we should do: for this we need virtue, experience and imagination. To draw an analogy with the game of tennis, it is not enough to know the rules or the aims, such as not to hit the ball out of play, to play well we need to learn the skills to be able to play a good rally. Similarly it is the experience and practice of trying to respect many different human values, together with a strong commitment never to betray any of these by doing wrong, makes us the sort of people who can face difficult situations well. It is the *virtuous* person who knows what to do in a difficult situation.

Teaching with Authority

And when Jesus finished these sayings, the crowds were astonished at his teaching, for he taught them as one who had authority, and not as their scribes. (Matthew 7:28-29)

What is the proper role for *authority* in morals? Authority does not mean the power to force someone to obey (as though the person obeying were just a well-trained animal). Authority, properly speaking, means that someone's word is itself a good reason for doing or believing something.

To give an example: Margaret is an authority on birds. Since she is very knowledgeable, it is reasonable to accept what she says on this subject. Occasionally she might make a mistake, and I might catch her out, but her word remains credible nonetheless. Some **expert authority** is like this, such as is the case with a wise counsellor. But there is another reason for having authorities on practical matters: if a group of people is going to do something together, it is very useful to put someone in charge. Some things can only get done if someone has overall responsibility for doing them. This kind of **political authority**, which belongs to whoever is in charge, also gives us a good reason to act - for the sake of respecting the common order of society. However, this is not always an over-riding reason: we should never do things that we ourselves know to be wrong.

The **authority of Jesus** was not a political authority in this sense, nor was it the authority of an expert who knows his subject. Jesus had authority from God. The authority of God is not like human authority, for God *cannot* make mistakes. God is all goodness and all truth, so if God tells us to do something, then we know that it must be the right thing to do. We should obey God, *not* because God is greater and stronger than we are, but because God is the best guide to what will truly fulfil us.

The authority which the **Catholic Church** has to teach on moral matters is not just a human authority (based on knowledge from experience) or a political authority (because the Church is a society) - though she has these kinds of authority as well. The authority of the Church to teach on moral matters comes directly from God, because the Church is founded on Jesus, who is God become man; and because the Holy Spirit, who is God present within us, continues to guide and guard the Church. When the Church teaches with her full authority, she teaches the word of God, which is, of its nature, true.

At the same time it is also important to stress that *not everything* that has been taught in the Catholic tradition has the same degree of authority. What has been taught solemnly by a Pope or an ecumenical council representing the whole Catholic Church, or what has been taught always and everywhere by all the bishops, is certain, true and infallible. However, many of the Church's teachings do not fall into this category.

Furthermore, the Church's understanding of the Gospel message has developed over time, under the guidance of the Holy Spirit. For instance, while slavery was never encouraged, the Church did at first tolerate it (the New Testament does not condemn the practice outright). Only later, in response to the appalling slave trade that developed in relatively modern times (from the sixteenth century), did the Church start to work actively for its complete abolition.

How then can we find out what is essential teaching and what is changeable? The **Creeds of the Church** concentrate on matters of faith, not on moral matters - because in the past the Church's moral teachings were not greatly disputed. Perhaps, in the future, creeds will be drawn up that explicitly involve moral truths. For now, there already exist some important Church documents on moral and social teaching; and, of course, we must also consider the moral and social teaching present in the Bible, as it is understood by the Catholic tradition.

There are certain points that are so central to the Catholic moral tradition that they must be considered *essential* and *unchangeable*, such as the Christian virtues of faith, hope and love, and the absolute prohibition on adultery, killing the innocent, and worshipping false gods. In doubtful matters the first question to ask is not "Do I agree with this teaching?" but rather "Is this teaching from God?", and then "How can I understand this teaching in the light of the whole tradition?"

If some proposition is only part of the changeable *expression* of the Gospel, then it *may* need to be re-expressed in some other way. However, even here, we must still give weight to the authority of the Church and support those who have the difficult job of leading.

The Pope or bishop has a duty to make particular decisions for the sake of the common good - such as appointing pastors, disciplining erring theologians, or settling disputes concerning faith or morals. Although such actions may be changeable - unlike the Church's most solemn moral teaching - they must still be respected for their public, legal and positive force, and should always be obeyed as far as we are able.

Honest Relationships

But from the beginning of creation, "God made them male and female." For this reason "a man shall leave his father and mother and be joined to his wife, and the two shall become one flesh." So they are no longer two but one flesh. What therefore God has joined together, let not man put asunder. (Mark 10:6-9)

We come into the world through the union of our mother and father. Even if we do not know either of our parents, they are still part of our story and identity. We learn from our immediate family how to speak and relate to others.

Family ties, especially those between parents and children, and brothers and sisters, are very strong by nature. This does not mean that we always get on easily with our families. The more we share ourselves with others, the more easily we can hurt one another. With friends we can put on a good show, but our family sees us as we are - at our worst, as well as at our best. Family ties are not freely chosen by us, but they are *part* of us, whether we like it or not; and the first task of a human being is to learn to live in and with his or her family. It is in this environment that we learn to relate to others and come to mature self-knowledge.

Becoming a parent gives both the mother and the father a new responsibility. Even if the child was unforeseen, he or she is still the child of these two people. **Parenthood** is a natural role, which - like being human itself - shapes our interests and duties. It is not only a matter of supplying a child's material needs, but also of accepting them as a person and trying to form a good relationship through which both parent and child can develop. It is wrong to set out to conceive a child if the mother and father are genuinely unable to cope with the responsibilities of parenthood; but, once conceived, every child must be cherished.

Others can help us in the job of **rearing and educating** - relatives, childminders, teachers - but it is the duty, and therefore the *right*, of parents first and foremost to bring up their child according to their own understanding. Children also have a duty to obey and learn from their parents. The city, tribe or state has no right to come between parent and child unless the child is in serious danger. Sometimes a parent who cannot cope will give up a child for **adoption**; and accepting a child for adoption can be a great act of love. While being brought up by another family makes for difficulties, especially during adolescence when the child is trying to establish his or her own identity, it is certainly better than being brought up in an institution without any sense of belonging to a family.

We all grow up in a family, and may eventually find someone we wish to live with as husband or wife, in order to start a family of our own. The Catholic Church recognises marriage as a human good common to all peoples, but sees Christian marriage as having an extra dimension - a lifelong sacramental bond. Jesus said that anyone who divorces and marries again is being unfaithful to the first and true marriage (*Mark* 10:11-12).

Separation may be necessary in extreme situations, but the Church does not recognise divorce and remarriage as an option for baptised Christian spouses, if their marriage was fully consummated and valid. However, if there was something deficient from the beginning, then it might not have been a valid marriage; and, after investigation, the Church might give the couple a declaration of nullity, or "annulment".

Then both partners would be free to marry others. There is something noble in companionship between people of the same sex, which might reasonably be given some legal protection, for example in relation to financial or healthcare decisions, but should be clearly separated from sexual or romantic love. Advocating the legal recognition of "same-sex marriage" seriously threatens the public understanding of marriage, the family and children, and further undermines the sanity of the common culture in the area of human sexuality. As argued earlier, sexual expression finds its proper human context only within the bond of heterosexual marriage, and when sexual communion is open to the blessing of children. An infertile married couple may still be *open* to children, but the sterility of homosexual intercourse is an *essential aspect* of the kind of act it is. The focus of the rights of couples, including homosexual couples, has also reversed the proper order of consideration in relation to adoption. The first prerequisite must be the good of each child and not the desire or putative right of adults to adopt. It is wrong for Government to force agencies to place children with individuals or couples where they do not think it in the best interest of the child to do so.

Extended family ties - with cousins, aunts and uncles - are less significant these days in modern Western societies like Britain. The State has taken over the provision of healthcare, education and public order, and has a much greater influence on our lives than it once did. Most people do not now work in family businesses. The idea of loyalty to an extended family has also been undermined by changes in the way we live. However, loyalty is still an important human virtue, and people do also get a sense of belonging from their profession, town, region, or particular "sub-culture" (defined by religion, common interest or ethnic background). **Loyalty** can easily degenerate into unfairness or prejudice towards "outsiders". In order to be healthy, loyalty must always be combined with **openness** and generosity, so that the knowledge that we belong gives us the confidence to accept others.

It is important to be able to get on well with others in the workplace, because difficult personal relationships can make it very hard to work well together. Nonetheless, good business relations - *friendships of mutual usefulness* - are not friendships in the deeper sense. More important are the relationships we have with people whom we spontaneously like and whose company we enjoy. However, these *friendships* of pleasant company, important as they are for us, still do not answer our basic need for serious friendship. True friendship, something that we cannot have with more than a few people, involves a shared life of common commitment to the true good of one another.

Aristotle called this the "friendship of virtue"; St Aelred of Rievaulx called it "spiritual friendship". Perhaps most of our friendships are a mix of more than one of these categories but the deepest friendship, **true friendship** is a very great human good.

The Kingdom of God

*P*ray then like this: Our Father who art in heaven, Hallowed be thy name. Thy kingdom come. Thy will be done, on earth as it is in heaven. (*Matthew* 6:9-10)

The aim of the Christian life is to find happiness in friendship with God, by the grace of God. This friendship, which involves faith, hope, and the love of God, also involves a commitment to love our neighbours, and even our enemies, as God loves them. The **kingdom** that we are working for is "a kingdom of truth and life, a kingdom of holiness and grace, a kingdom of justice, love and peace" (Roman Missal). Therefore we should seek to build a fair and just society, and should care especially for the poor and the socially excluded. Jesus said, "Whatever you do to one of the least of these, my brothers and sisters, you do to me" (*Matthew* 25:40).

Jesus preached the coming of the kingdom of God, but he also gathered a people together, appointed twelve apostles, and founded the **Church**. Within the Church, we read about the acts and teaching of Jesus in the Gospels, and hear about him in the other parts of the Bible. We also share in the very life of Jesus when we are baptised with water, when we eat and drink his body and blood in the Mass, and when we receive the other sacraments.

The Church is a visible society and, in addition to the moral law, she has her own canon law, for the spiritual good of her members. Catholics are bound to fulfil the old Sabbath law by keeping the Lord's day (Sunday), and certain major feasts, as "holy days" - by going to Mass and abstaining from work that would inhibit rest, celebration or the due worship of God. We are also bound to support the clergy, practise penance at the appropriate times, confess our sins to a priest and receive Holy Communion at least once a year, and marry (if we choose to marry) according to the laws of the Church. Canon law exists to promote our spiritual good, but it cannot of itself bring about unity. It is only the presence of the Holy Spirit that creates the bond of unity and peace.

It is the same Holy Spirit who gives us the hope of really making a difference, and doing something worthwhile with our time on earth. Faced with the immense problems and suffering of the world, and with our own obvious weaknesses, it would be easy to despair, and turn instead to following the crowd, our routine, or our immediate impulses. The message of the Gospel is that our hope rests not in ourselves, but in the God who made us and who has already achieved the decisive victory, in the life, death and Resurrection of Jesus. Thankfully, it does not rest on our shoulders to save the world, but only to play our part in the great work of God, who is, all the time, healing and redeeming his creation.

The first step for each one of us is to acknowledge the vanity of trying to find happiness on our own, and accept the help that is offered to us. Only by realising the constancy and infinite depth of God's love can we be given the courage to face our failings honestly, confess them explicitly, and, with the help of God, turn from them.

Confession and faith in God liberates us to hope, without the dishonesty of pride or self-deception. Then we can ask what plans God has in mind for us, by which we can find happiness through serving others. Every human being is called to love God and to find salvation, but the particular way of life to which each of us is destined (our calling or Vocation) is unique. Some are called to great and heroic efforts to preach the faith in the face of danger, or in fighting against injustice for the sake of God's children. No one is exempt from helping in this struggle; but for many of us the way of life to which we are called will be humble and seemingly ordinary, rather than dramatic. It will be through married life, through teaching music, mending drains, shuffling paperwork, or managing a team of workers, that most of us will find happiness, if it is to be found. What makes each of these works a vocation is both the choice of work, how we each hear our call to serve society, and, equally important, the way in which we carry out this work, the love and care with which we live and work with one another, and the honesty of our relationships with God and our neighbours. In this way Christians can become witnesses in their work, in the NHS, in schools, shops, and offices, just by quietly living their jobs as well as possible, humanly and effectively.

We should not think of the moral life as a set of rules that restrict our freedom and stop us from doing what we want to do. We should think of it as the fulness of life, the worthwhile life, through which we can find ourselves, and gain a respect for ourselves and for others. Because of our weakness, this is only possible with God's help, which he gives to us through his Son Jesus our Saviour, and the Holy Spirit, who is our life and inspiration. Whatever our talents and goals may be, whatever it is that really attracts us (and that we can see to be truly good), we will find fulfilment only with God and not apart from God. Rebellion against God is rebellion against reality.

There is a path that God has for us, through which we can find our happiness. What is required of us is to walk this path - not seeing the whole journey, but at every step putting our trust in God. Ultimately all worldly goods will fail, our friends will die, and we too will face death; but if we have trusted in God in life, then we may trust that, even in death, he will bring us to the life of the resurrection, where Jesus awaits us, and where everything we have lost will be restored.

Catholic Truth Society
40-46 Harleyford Road, London SE11 5AY

website: *CTSbooks.org*

CTS Code: D821

ISBN: 978 1 78469 185 1

Acknowledgements

This volume has been compiled from material previously published under the following titles: *Handbook of Novenas to the Saints*, first published 2010 by The Incorporated Catholic Truth Society; Copyright © 2010, 2017 The Incorporated Catholic Truth Society. *Little Book of Litanies*, first published 2016 by The Incorporated Catholic Truth Society; © 2016 The Incorporated Catholic Truth Society. *Novena to the Holy Spirit*, first published 2006 by The Incorporated Catholic Truth Society; Copyright © 2006 The Incorporated Catholic Truth Society. *Living Life to the Full*, third edition first published 2013 by The Incorporated Catholic Truth Society; © The Incorporated Catholic Truth Society 2013. First published May 2001. Second edition July 2001. *The Secret of Joy*, first published 2005 by The Incorporated Catholic Truth Society; Copyright © 2005 The Incorporated Catholic Truth Society, in this translated text. *Confirmation: The Spirit of Christ*, first published 2004 by The Incorporated Catholic Truth Society; Copyright © 2004 The Incorporated Catholic Truth Society. *Marian Prayer Book*, first published 2012 by The Incorporated Catholic Truth Society, Compilation and design © 2012 The Incorporated Catholic Truth Society. Excerpts from the English translation of The Roman Missal © 2010, International Commission on English in the Liturgy Corporation (ICEL); excerpts from the English translation of The Liturgy of the Hours © 1974, ICEL; excerpts from the English translation of Holy Communion & Worship of the Eucharist outside Mass © 1974, ICEL; excerpt from the English translation of Rite of Penance © 1974, ICEL. All rights reserved. Latin text © Libreria Editrice Vaticana, Vatican City State, 2008. Concordat cum originali: Martin Foster (England and Wales). Permission granted for distribution in the dioceses of Scotland.